WARRIOR WOMEN: REMAKING POSTSECONDARY PLACES THROUGH RELATIONAL NARRATIVE INQUIRY

ADVANCES IN RESEARCH ON TEACHING

Series Editor: Volumes 1–11: Jere Brophy
Volumes 12–16: Stefinee Pinnegar

Recent Volumes:

ADVANCES IN RESEARCH ON TEACHING   VOLUME 17

WARRIOR WOMEN: REMAKING POSTSECONDARY PLACES THROUGH RELATIONAL NARRATIVE INQUIRY

BY

MARY ISABELLE YOUNG
Faculty of Education, University of Winnipeg, Winnipeg, Manitoba, Canada

LUCY JOE
*Membertou First Nation, Membertou School (Maupeltu Kina'matno'kuom),
Membertou, Nova Scotia, Canada*

JENNIFER LAMOUREUX
Seven Oaks School Division, Winnipeg, Manitoba, Canada

LAURA MARSHALL
*Eskasoni Mi'kmaw Nation, Eskasoni Elementary & Middle School, Eskasoni,
Nova Scotia, Canada*

SISTER DOROTHY MOORE
*Membertou First Nation, Education Department, Membertou; Elder-in-Residence,
Cape Breton University, Sydney, Nova Scotia, Canada*

JERRI-LYNN ORR
Aboriginal Community Campus, Winnipeg, Manitoba, Canada

BRENDA MARY PARISIAN
Peguis First Nation, Peguis Central School, Peguis, Manitoba, Canada

KHEA PAUL
*Eskasoni Mi'kmaw Nation, Allison M. Bernard Memorial High School,
Eskasoni, Nova Scotia, Canada*

FLORENCE PAYNTER
*Manitoba First Nations Education Resource Centre; Elder-in-Residence at
Migiizii Agamik, University of Manitoba, Winnipeg, Manitoba, Canada*

JANICE HUBER
Faculty of Education, University of Regina, Regina, Saskatchewan, Canada

With a foreword by Marie Battiste
With an afterword by D. Jean Clandinin

Emerald

United Kingdom – North America – Japan
India – Malaysia – China

Emerald Group Publishing Limited
Howard House, Wagon Lane, Bingley BD16 1WA, UK

First edition 2012
Second edition 2015

British Library Cataloguing in Publication Data
A catalogue record for this book is available from the British Library

ISBN: 978-1-78560-437-9
ISSN: 1479-3687 (Series)

ISOQAR certified
Management Systems,
awarded to Emerald for
adherence to Quality
and Environmental
standards ISO 9001:2008
and 14001:2004,
respectively

Certificate Number 1985
ISO 9001
ISO 14001

INVESTOR IN PEOPLE

CONTENTS

TESTIMONIALS

Warrior Women: Remaking Post-Secondary Places through Relational Narrative Inquiry is a book unlike any other I have read. The book draws from the voices of 10 women with diverse narrative histories who come to walk alongside one another as warriors "in a more than 500 year struggle for equity and justice for Aboriginal people in Canada" (Young et al., 2012). The book is alive and moving, making tangible the oral storytelling devices "rhythm, repetition and ritual" of which Sewall (1996) speaks, and which resound to create an embodied sense of how intergenerational narratives shape both backward and forward looking stories. The stories compel and as the authors call us to hear the beating of the drum, they likewise urgently invite us to see our own place in joining hands, in walking alongside, and in co-composing ways forward into the world together. Such new stories, stories such as theirs, give we readers hope that new possible intergenerational narrative reverberations *can be* co-composed."

— Pam Steeves, Adjunct Professor,
Centre for Research for Teacher Education & Development,
University of Alberta

"By courageously beginning in their own storied lives, the authors provide insights into intergenerational narrative reverberations of colonization and residential schools. In so doing, these warrior women call each of us, Canadian and non-Canadian, Aboriginal and non-Aboriginal, young and old, female and male, to consider how our lives, our beliefs, our attitudes, our taken-for-grantedness (Greene, 2005) are contributing to these intergenerational narrative reverberations. This book shows that to deny the scars, past and present, resulting from colonization and residential schools is to ensure their continuance into (or onto) future generations.

— Marilyn Huber, Policy Research,
Alberta Ministry of Education

ACKNOWLEDGEMENTS

Engaging in this long-term, intensely relational narrative inquiry was not easy work; we have been deeply supported in so many differing ways and wish to express our gratitude.

We are grateful to our families, and our ancestors, for all of the many ways their support has contributed to our abilities to sustain our participation in our narrative inquiry and our completion of our book. We know our seven years of making this book is a long time and we are deeply grateful for your patience and love.

We are grateful to Marie and Jean for their careful, thoughtful travelling to our worlds which so profoundly shows in their respective foreword and afterword. We are deeply honoured by the presence of each of you, also warrior women, whose living and writing has been central in our journey together.

We are grateful to Marilyn Huber, Shaun Murphy and Pam Steeves for their careful listening all the way along and for their reading and responding to final drafts of our book. Thank you for keeping us believing in ourselves! We are also grateful to our many additional friends at the Centre for Research for Teacher Education and Development, University of Alberta, people who so humbly live out understandings that 'sometimes a person needs a story more than food to stay alive' (Lopez, 1993, p. 60).

We are grateful to Chloe Mustooch for her work to create the perfect image for the front cover of our book. Thank you for taking time to hear stories of each of us so that as you created this image you felt our energy. Thank you to Vera Caine and to Sean Lessard for introducing Chloe to us.

We are grateful to numerous colleagues at St. Francis Xavier University and the Universities of Regina and Winnipeg for the ways they supported us during this journey. Thank you for honouring our requests to utilize the research time stipends we received from SSHRC and our requests for research terms and sabbaticals. Thank you also to the financial services department of the University of Winnipeg for all of your expertise and support with the distribution of the money involved with the grant that supported this work.

We are grateful to Stefinee Pinnegar, Chris Hart and Sophie Barr whom we worked alongside at Emerald. From the first moment when Stefinee invited us to consider Emerald as the publisher for this book we have felt deeply honoured and respected. Thank you for trusting us.

We are grateful to Lauren Starko of Comma Police who carefully edited and formatted our book as it was in the making. Thank you, also, for your support along the way.

We are grateful to the Social Sciences and Humanities Research Council of Canada (SSHRC) from whom we received funding which supported our relational narrative inquiry. Without this funding this work, our relationships and this book would not have happened. Thank you also for the two extensions you granted to us so that we could do this work in good ways.

We say 'Welalio' ... 'Kitchi Miigwetch' ... 'Thank you'.

We dedicate our stories to all of the Aboriginal children, youth, and adult students who are or will navigate school and university contexts.

We also dedicate our stories to all the warrior women who came before us and those yet to come.

We know you are yearning, waiting, for all of us to walk together in good ways.

GROUP PHOTO FROM WINNIPEG FALL 2008

Winnipeg, 2008

Back row left to right: Lucy Joe, Janice Huber, Mary Isabelle Young,
                            Jean Clandinin, Brenda Mary Parisian,
                            Jerri-Lynn Orr, Khea Paul, Jennifer
                            Lamoureux, Laura (Lulu) Marshall
Front row left to right: Florence Paynter, Sister Dorothy Moore

FOREWORD TO WARRIOR WOMEN

It was at the Canadian Association for the Study of Indigenous Education in 2010 in Concordia University that I first heard from the women who were part of this study. They lined up in the front of the room in desks to share each their part of what would become the foundation of this book. The topic was their post-secondary education experiences becoming a teacher. Among them were a few of my Mi'kmaw relatives and long time friends. I remembered two of them as youth in Eskasoni when I lived there. The story they told was familiar. It was at the kitchen tables that I first heard about the experiences of these Mi'kmaq youth going to school off reserve. The traumatic events were regaled over and over, and everyone had stories to share about the racism they experienced taking the bus to the nearby town to go to high school, and the coached determination they received to continue going to school everyday. By the time graduation came each year, the buses that were filled at the beginning of the school year emptied out, and at most a handful of determined steadfast students graduated.

Mi'kmaq daily life is like that, filled with stories as people relive their lives together – the mundane, the joyous, and the traumatic, all part of the manifestations of Indigenous community knowledge. The kitchen table over tea and luskinigan, a Mi'kmaw bread, has a way of encouraging these stories out, and everyone who enters a house in our communities knows there will be tea and talk and no judgment in the stories they tell. We gently tease out these thoughts. Everyone vies for her turn to tell a story that will capture attention and may, as befitting the moment, end in a good laugh. These storytelling events are the best parts of living in family and in community.

Each generation finds meaning for their lives through the stories they tell and the meaning making it creates for them. Ultimately these stories become a source forging expressive creativity, for shaping identities, and making decisions about our lives. Many stories are not shared among youth, however, as they represent events that replay traumas, struggles, and disappointments that require safe spaces, quiet encouraging spaces, with friends, family, and loved ones who share their pain. Such has been the reason why the Truth and Reconciliation Commission is making its way through Canada to help those now-older students speak their truths and to share that period of their lives with a wider audience.

Being able to connect consistently to the inner forces of the self is one way that learners can each seek actively to achieve optimally their life journey. And narratives do that for us. It is about the ability to understand the capacities and lessons needed to learn on a life path. It is knowing one's self fully and holistically and ability to reflect and vision forward the life journey that enables and creates certain skills, talents, or propensities. It is about feeling free and open to express the inner spirit and its magnet like attractions that help us to become who we are. Shared story telling and active listening in safe nonjudgmental places are important to how this process unfolds.

What educators and teachers might learn in this book about the experiences of these women is found in their shared memories of their going to schools across Canada. It is to be found in the stories of those youth whose lives unfolded each in different ways to choose to become teachers. Their preparation has not been just the teaching methods they took or the books they read, but their shared knowing of what makes for success in their students' lives by sharing with each other their own experiences. Their stories are about the learning spirit that frames a broader concept than formal education provides in skills and knowledge. It is about constructing their sense of reality and making sense of the sensory input to find a distinctive life journey dedicated to teaching, working with youth, and helping them through difficult times.

As each generation in Canada has today had the experience of an education, for good or bad, these stories reverberate common themes that center diverse experiences in a landscape of qualitative research. The researchers of this study, Mary Young and Janice Huber, set out to identify how the voices of generations of Canadian women, as students, are revealed through stories, and what stories they are living with, within, between, and across generations. As they engage in one of the most natural habituated cultural processes of every culture, storytelling, we are given a portal through which we view critical events in their situated lives. Narrative inquiry research offers an important process. Beyond the researchers, research questions, proposals, partnerships, shared responsibilities, taped recordings, transcripts, and collaborations, are stories that in their richness are taken out in print to be shared and appreciated, like those at the kitchen table.

The book situates stories of women who have succeeded in education, although that trajectory through elementary school or residential school or university classrooms is not one that came with cultural or economic privilege from belonging to the dominant languages and cultures. Rather the experiences these women relay are initially marked by difference from the privileged groups, perceived deficiency in their language capacities, and contexts that present challenges to their long-term aspiration for success. In each story is a voice that reveals from many relationships and diverse contexts a piece of the world in which we live. Each gives us a point of reference to take up our own story about our identities, belonging, marked exclusions, alienation, determination, and successes all framed by situations and contexts that reveal the beauty and resilience of the learning spirit. But their stories speak to me most vividly about the continuing need for decolonizing of education without which continues to diminish the opportunities for youth in Canada and beyond.

Marie Battiste
University of Saskatchewan, Canada

CHAPTER 1

NOT TOMORROW ... TODAY

Corridors
Long
Empty
Silent

Doors closed
Through small windows
See desks in rows

Podium
Prominent
At front

Person lecturing
Need to take notes
This knowledge
The answer

You don't know
We'll teach you
Silence

See only
Backs of heads
Individualistic
Disconnected
From self
From one another
Layers of denial
Only focus
Highest marks
Surviving
Getting through
Being done
Having a degree
Making money
Successful me
(Word image composed from Mary's & Janice's remembered post-secondary experiences
written in fall, 2006)

A Moment With My Ancestors

As hard
As Pine Creek residential school
Had been
In 1967–68
At least I did not hear comments
Like those I heard
In 1968-69
At St. Charles Academy
Which were
"Those girls from the reserve are dumb"
After a while
I started to take it all in
The only way to deal with it
Was to internalize it
I did not tell anyone how I was feeling
I never thought of asking the other girls
If they felt the same way
The more I thought about the comment
The more I believed it
I was not doing very well academically
I did not like myself at times
I think I actually hated myself
I was fat
I was carrying around the extra weight
I put on at Pine Creek residential school
The year before

I had always enjoyed school
But I was beginning to dislike it a lot
I would tell myself that I could not quit
I told myself
I was the one who wanted to come to school
And no matter what happens
I am going to finish what I started
I was 15 years old

I went home that year
And for the first time in my life
I felt dejected
I was a failure
I could not bear the thought
Of going home
And telling EVERYBODY
That I
Too
Had failed
I was embarrassed

And ashamed
I had always done well in school
And EVERYBODY
Knew that to be the case
I never thought of myself
As being dumb
Nor did I think
That I might fail a grade
I simply did not know
What to do
With these feelings
I did not try to explain
To anyone
What may have contributed
To my failure
Because I thought
It would sound
Too much
Like an excuse
The more I tried to understand what had happened
The more depressed I became

My mother was more objective
She told me to try again
I have come to understand the history
Of the residential school system
And my mother would have known
I had to go back to school
She was probably fearful
To not send me back
Her words were not comforting
And I retreated into my shell
Continuing
To feel sorry for myself
I could not accept
The fact
That I had failed my Grade 10
I spent most of the summer
Trying to figure out
What I had done wrong

The Indian agent came to Bloodvein
A couple of times over the summer of 1969
He wanted to know
What I was going to do
About school
I told him
I was never

Going to go back to school
And at the time
I think
I really meant it
I had convinced myself
Perhaps there was no way
I was going to get
My high school diploma
But there was a part of me
That I could not ignore
I kept telling myself
I had to go back to school
I know I can do it!

There was a rock formation
About 400 yards
From my parents' home
It sloped down to the river
And that is where
I would go
To think
There was a perfect place
Where I would sit
And let my legs dangle
Into the water
It was
At this place
That I would contemplate
My future
As I write this
I can still feel
The warm water
Between my toes
One afternoon
As I sat there
I felt an energy
I cannot describe
All I know
Is I felt it
Throughout my body
It felt
Strong
Energizing
And I felt
Rejuvenated
I knew then
That my ancestors
Had been there

Before me
They came
To tell me something

When the Indian agent came back
I told him
I would go back to school
On one condition
And that was
To return
To the same school
He said
"I thought you hated that school?"
I told him
I did
But I had to go back
To that school
So I could put
Myself
Back together again

Naayapikang[1]
Which is the name
Of the rock formation
Continues to be
My special place
Whenever I need solace
I go there
Spiritually
To feel
Ancestral energy
(Word image composed from Mary's story written on October 16, 2008)

Remembering Where I Am From

It was well past midnight
On the New Year's Eve
I am remembering
Smoke from the fire slowly threaded upward
Through a natural chimney shaped by the circular opening at the tops of the trees
Stars shone beyond
Coyotes howled
We were enveloped by ancient trees
Boughs of spruce hanging low
Heavy with snow
Even though it was a winter night in northern Alberta
We were still gathered around the fire
Telling stories
Remembering other times

People and places
Teasing and laughing

As the hours moved into the next day, the next year
The group of people grew smaller
My dad talked then as he often did
About the blessings of this place and our way of life
Lives
Textured by knowing that our survival was intimately connected
With the land and water
The animals
And people
Who shaped and sustained us
He also, again, like so many earlier times in my life
Reminded my siblings and me
To not forget where we are from

In those early morning moments
And in many of the moments I experienced in this place where the spruce
    stretched to the sky
I grew in understanding my privilege in knowing and loving this place
My parents began bringing my siblings and me, family and community members
To this "spruce tree" place
When I was a young child
On summer days as the sun shot through openings between the boughs of the
    towering spruce or the leaves of the poplar trees
Bright shifting patterns formed on the grass
To stand in this circle of trees in the fall was to experience a kaleidoscope of color
When it rained or snowed we were protected

As a young adult
I left these spruce trees and the animals, people, and situations I experienced in
    this rural northern place when I moved to a large urban centre to attend
    a teacher education program
In this transition
Not only was I at substantial physical distance from where I am from
But I was also
At substantial distance from the kinds of experiences that shaped my early years
My early identity

In the university place where I studied
The knowing I carried of humility, respect, and courage and commitment to fight
    for the healthy survival of land, water, animals, and people
Did not seem to matter
Instead
What always seemed to matter
Most
Was the amount of knowledge I could read
Remember

And show
Usually
On multiple choice tests
In this context
I learned to compete for the highest grades and to silence the callings I felt to pay
    attention
To particularities
Relationships
And responsibilities

After my dad had passed over 2 years
My mom decided to move from this rural northern place
This was a painful decision and transition
For my mom
Who had lived there for over 45 years
It was also painful for my siblings and me
As we listened to our mom and thought about her future life and each of our
    future lives
Some months after this place was sold to another person
He called my mom
He had many questions about the spruce tree place
He could tell this place had been loved and that people had spent much time there
When my mom explained that it was a family gathering place
And that she and my dad were in the process of turning it into a wildlife sanctuary
    when my dad became ill and then died
He told my mom that in the years ahead
My family was always welcome to spend time there

I was
At that time
Living in eastern Canada
A place I am now from as an adult
I am immensely grateful to this person
Because as a teacher in Alberta and then as a teacher educator in Nova Scotia
I spent much time in this place on the week-ends and in the summers
It was a place that sustained me
A place that kept me wakeful to where I am from
Wakeful to remembering
The land
Water
Animals
And people
Who shaped my early life
My early identity

Today
I realize
These relationships still shape what and how I know and who I am and who I am
    becoming

As I interact with children, youth, families, colleagues, beginning and experienced
    educators, and community members
And, in these interactions as I am called to remember where I am from
I am simultaneously called to wonder
And to want to know
Something
Of where others are from
Past
And present
(Word image composed from Janice's story written on October 16, 2008)

We begin with these three word images as a way to show something of the central exploration of our book: the significant connections between place and identity in being and becoming Aboriginal teachers. The first word image, drawn from Mary's and Janice's memories of experiences lived in post-secondary contexts, shows the disconnections they often felt in these places, disconnections from themselves, disconnections from the people who sat beside them in the desks and rows, disconnections from the dominant ways and focuses of learning. In their experiences in these post-secondary places, connection was not what mattered. Instead, attention seemed focused on surviving, getting through, getting done; often, this focus shaped competition for the highest marks, that is, to be the best. In being the best success was guaranteed, success as determined through future salaries and possessions.

Janice's and Mary's memories of the people, places, knowledge, and relationships they carried into these post-secondary places are startling alongside this first word image. As Mary made visible in her story of the energy she felt as she sat at *naayapikang*, the learning she experienced in this sacred place is a way to honour her ancestors, the teachings of her mother and father, and relationships with family. Being in this place Mary knew who she was and found strength and energy to continue with the experiences ahead. Janice's connections with a place where she grew up were nurtured alongside her parents, siblings, and neighbors and the land, water, and animals from which they were sustained. Her dad's reminder to not forget where she is from became a resonant voice in her life, reminding her to live by, to respect, this early place and these early relationships.

Mary's and Janice's storied experiences are a way to show something of the deep connections they carry of place(s) and who they are becoming, connections that pulse in their bodies, in their identities. Alongside their word image of remembered post-secondary places, Janice's and Mary's experiences raise significant questions about post-secondary contexts, questions such as: Why are post-secondary contexts often experienced as places where individuals' strengths are not recognized? Why do post-secondary places often seem focused on reshaping or remaking people? What might be different in post-secondary places if people's identities were valued and nurtured?

As Mary and Janice puzzled over these questions they were drawn to the understandings of Leslie Marmon Silko (1996) who speaks of the Pueblo potters who in their creation of "petroglyphs and oral narratives" would never have thought to separate themselves "from the earth and sky" (p. 27). She writes that

> As long as the human consciousness remains *within* the hills, canyons, cliffs, and the plants, clouds, and sky, the term *landscape*, as it has entered the English language, is misleading. 'A portion of territory the eye can comprehend in a single view' does not correctly describe the relationship between the human being and his or her surroundings. This assumes the viewer is somehow *outside* or *separate* from the territory she or he surveys. Viewers are as much a part of the landscape as the boulders they stand on. (Italics in original, 1996, p. 27)

Bringing Marmon Silko's understandings of the relational aspects of place and identity alongside their remembered experiences of post-secondary landscapes shaped Janice's and Mary's imaginings of how different life in post-secondary places *could be* if the people who entered onto these landscapes were invited into spaces where their lives mattered. What might be different in post-secondary experiences if students were encouraged to remember the people, places, and experiences they are from and, in turn, had opportunities to attend to and inquire into the shaping and reshaping of their identities while navigating post-secondary places? What new narratives for composing lives in post-secondary places might open up? In particular Mary and Janice were drawn toward wonders about what might be different for people of Aboriginal[2] ancestry as they navigate Canadian post-secondary places.

1.1. A NARRATIVE OF COLONIZATION STRETCHING BACKWARD AND FORWARD

In a paper shared at the 2004 Canadian Society for the Study of Education (CSSE), Marie Battiste urged Canadian academics and policy makers to become part of a transformative process of reconstructing Canada's colonial education system which she describes as shaping "Indigenous peoples' trauma and disconnection with many aspects of education and themselves"

(p. 2). Battiste calls for the repositioning of Indigenous knowledges in post-secondary institutions, a process through which institutional structures and practices, curriculum foundations, and traditions are substantially changed and, in particular, that these are changed in ways that value and engage the capacities of Aboriginal students. Battiste's argument is significant for both Aboriginal post-secondary students and for their communities.

As highlighted in the Assembly of *First Nations Post-Secondary Education Review* (i.e. Mi'kmaw Kina'matnewey, 2000): "Education of First Nations students not only provides the opportunity for students to achieve their full potential, but it also provides the opportunity for them to make a contribution to their communities" (p. 2). Post-secondary education funding, however, is "failing to meet rising tuition and living costs" for Aboriginal students attending post-secondary institutions (Mi'kmaq Kina'matnewey, 2000, p. 30). Not only are Aboriginal post-secondary students facing pressing financial struggles, but they often also experience a lack of support for Indigenous programming and structures in the post-secondary places they attend. Some Aboriginal post-secondary students fear that in speaking out about their experiences the little support they currently feel will be taken away (Augustine, 2002). While in 2000, Castellano, Davis, and Lahache showed that from 1981 to 1996 the "gap between Aboriginal and non-Aboriginal university completions has grown from just over 7 percent to 11 percent" (p. 172), this gap continues to widen. Indeed, a 2009 report released by The Canadian Council on Learning indicated that "7.7% of the Aboriginal population had attained a university credential, while 23.4% of the non-Aboriginal population had university attainment" (p. 9). Similar statistics released in 2010 by the Canadian Centre for Policy Alternatives report that

> there remains a significant gap in the number of Aboriginal peoples obtaining a Bachelor's degree – 8% of Aboriginal peoples have a bachelor degree or higher – and the rest of Canadians – 22%... . Educational attainment among Aboriginal peoples still lags well behind averages for the Canadian population as a whole. Non-Aboriginal Canadians are far more likely to complete high school and to get a university degree and the gap between the groups is growing. (Wilson & Macdonald, 2010, p. 4)

A fundamental feature of this report is its focus on the growing economic inequities among Aboriginal and non-Aboriginal people in Canada. Holding in the foreground the increasing poverty experienced by Aboriginal people shows that regardless of educational attainment, unless the Government of Canada takes seriously the need to move from a paternalistic to a reconciliatory approach to all matters in relation with Aboriginal people, little will change.

> Sadly, the Government of Canada appears committed to the colonial administration of Aboriginal communities, perhaps best evidenced by the continued application of the *Indian Act*, fundamentally unchanged since 1876. It is the belief that others know what is good for peoples who have suffered under colonial rule – and continue to do so – that must be abandoned. (Wilson & Macdonald, 2010, p. 26)

As described by Battiste (2004), in the context of what later became Canada, the "contact of Aboriginal peoples with European peoples" was, initially, cooperative and respectful, "with Europeans depending on the various nations to help them find sustenance, shelter, and advice about their way around the continent" (p. 4). Yet, as time passed and the Europeans "felt more comfortable, they resorted to the values and hierarchy of their own traditions and their own origins and forced the people they encountered into slavery and subjugation" (p. 4). In time, as the dominant social narrative shifted from respectful relationships to oppression, changes were felt in every aspect of the lives of Aboriginal people in Canada, including their schooling experiences. As part of the Treaty-making process across Canada, Aboriginal people negotiated with the Europeans for schools that would support Aboriginal children to flourish. The schools, however, eventually "deteriorated into oppressive residential schools built on negative stereotypical mythic representations of Indians and Indian society and Eurocentric glorification" (p. 5).

According to the Royal Commission on Aboriginal People (1996):

> Education is seen as the vehicle for both enhancing the life of the individual and reaching collective goals.... As well, consistent with Aboriginal traditions, education must develop the whole child, intellectually, spiritually, emotionally and physically.... However, rather than nurturing the individual, schooling experiences typically erode identity and self-worth. (pp. 433–434)

The Commission concluded that the

> Destiny of a people is intricately bound to the ways its children are educated. Education is the transmission of cultural DNA from one generation to the next. It shapes the language and pathways of thinking, the contours of character and values, the social skills and creative potential of the individual. It determines the productive skills of a people. (p. 433)

Numerous scholars have written about ways the dominant historical, social, cultural, and institutional narratives which shape Canadian post-secondary contexts conflict with the differing knowledge and perspectives held by post-secondary students, communities, and Elders of First Nations,

Metís, and *Inuit* ancestry (Archibald & Urion, 1995; Kirkness & Barnhardt, 1991; Orr, Paul, & Paul, 2002; Stonechild, 2006; Tompkins, 2002; Young, 1997). Eber Hampton (1995), focusing on the experiences of students of Native American ancestry attending Harvard University, wrote that "brainwashing ... [occurs] when education is used to wipe out identity, language, culture, philosophy, and substitute something else for these" (p. 52). These tensions, however, are not localized to North America as "schooling and educational success remain elusive for disproportionately large numbers of Indigenous students in countries such as New Zealand, Australia, Alaska [USA], Hawaii ... and the Pacific Nations" (Menzies, Archibald, & Smith, 2004, p. 1).

Among the many understandings emerging from this scholarship on the past and continuing conflicting narratives often experienced by Aboriginal post-secondary students is the need for increased numbers of teachers of Aboriginal ancestry in Aboriginal, urban, and rural Canadian schools (Fitznor, 2002; St. Denis, 2010; Ward & Bouvier, 2001). Of particular concern within this literature is the fact that the numbers of Aboriginal teachers in Canadian schools remains low especially considering that the population of "Aboriginal young people is rapidly increasing, with an expectation that in the next 15 to 20 years, First Nations students will represent over 25 per cent of the elementary student population in some provinces and territories" (The Council of Ministers of Education, 2008, p. 1).

1.2. THINKING NARRATIVELY ABOUT LIVES IN POST-SECONDARY PLACES

Mary and Janice read the earlier described literature, which draws attention to the experiences of Aboriginal post-secondary students in Canada and around the world, prior to the beginning of our relational narrative inquiry (Clandinin & Connelly, 2000; Craig & Huber, 2007). Due to their interest in narrative inquiry and in thinking narratively about experience, about lives, in post-secondary places they gradually saw four key aspects as threading a grounding from which to begin a long-term relational narrative inquiry into the experiences of Aboriginal students in post-secondary places and their experiences of becoming teachers.

1.2.1. Aboriginal Education

In his redefinition of Indian education Hampton (1995) states that:

> Walking the circle of Indian education, facing the east, it is traditional to pray for our children. It is an Indian tradition – it is a deeply human tradition – to pray for future generations. Those traditions – those prayers, hopes and dreams of our Old Ones – mark as much as, perhaps more than, their defeats, their fears and their errors. To educate ourselves and our children, we must start with who we are, with the traditions, the values, and the ways of life we have absorbed as children of the people. An Elder told me, "I am just one day old." This day connects our past and future, the child within to the elder we hope to become. The identity of Indian people is that which links our history and our future to this day, now. (p. 22)

Hampton's earlier noted understandings of Aboriginal education shape an urgent call for something different within school systems as well as within post-secondary places. In his redefinition of the education of Aboriginal students, Hampton calls for learning that is significantly different from what Aboriginal students in post-secondary places typically experience. We understand the kind of learning which Hampton imagined, learning which is necessarily attentive to "the traditions, the values, and the ways of life we have absorbed as children of the people" (p. 22) as calling for education in which experience and story are central. Within his call Hampton shares his insights about the need for Aboriginal students to be supported to grow in understanding who they are and who they are becoming as they, in the present, link the histories of their people with generations past and future.

As *Anishinabe kwe*, Mary came to understand the importance of knowing who we are and where we come from. Part of Mary's becoming as an Aboriginal educator has been shaped by understanding the impact of the residential school system and how it eroded many of the traditions, values, and beliefs of which Hampton (1995) writes. As she reflected in her journal on this impact of the residential school system, Mary wondered how the legacy of the residential school system may continue to influence Aboriginal students who are now in post-secondary education:

> I have come to understand that, if we, as Aboriginal and non-Aboriginal educators, want to understand and acknowledge the experiences of Aboriginal students in university, we need to acknowledge and understand the development and purpose of the residential school system in Canada. If we are unable to do that, the education of Aboriginal people in Canada remains a void; a void we no longer can ignore. (Mary's written reflection, spring, 2004)

As Mary's reflection shows, she too, is calling for attention to experience and story in post-secondary learning. Central within the learning Mary imagines is attention to the ongoing legacy of the residential school system in the experiences, in the lives of Aboriginal people, past, present, and future; it is learning in which dominant social, cultural, familial, linguistic, and institutional narratives, past and present, need to be traced so that their impact, past, present, and into the future, can be understood. Without this kind of learning, Mary is concerned that the education of Aboriginal post-secondary students will remain "a void," that is, a process filled with learning likely empty of their experiences, of their lives and, as a result, empty of opportunities to understand ways in which the past continues to shape current experiences, lives, and situations in and outside of post-secondary places.

Collectively, we carried calls of the need for reshaping the learning experienced by Aboriginal students into our inquiry as we attended to the experiences of the six Aboriginal teachers who are co-researchers in this relational narrative inquiry – Brenda Mary Parisian, Jennifer Lamoureux, Jerri-Lynn Orr, Khea Paul, Lucy Joe, and Lulu (Laura) Marshall. In doing so, we tried to stay wakeful throughout our inquiry to possibilities of Aboriginal and non-Aboriginal educators and post-secondary students working in relation with one another, together learning how to walk in good ways (Young, 2003, 2005b) so that Aboriginal post-secondary students might experience learning in post-secondary places which no longer entails needing to give up or erase their identities.

1.2.2. Curriculum Making

When Michael Connelly and Jean Clandinin (1988) developed the idea of curriculum as the unfolding of life experiences, central within this understanding was their desire to shift attention from abstract concepts or objects (i.e., an outcome, a text book, etc.) toward what is being "experienced in situations" (p. 6). In this way, they called for curriculum to be understood from the vantage point of the people involved. Dewey's (1938) understanding of experience, particularly his attention to the intertwining of continuity, interaction, and situation, were significant in Connelly and Clandinin's re-visioning of curriculum as an interactive, unfolding process. Also woven into their re-visioning was Schwab's (1973) conception of four curriculum commonplaces: teacher, learner, subject matter, and milieu. Clandinin and Connelly (1992) subsequently drew attention to curriculum as a "curriculum of life," a vibrant process they described as:

> an account of teachers' and children's lives together in schools and classrooms ... [In this view of curriculum making] the teacher is seen as an integral part of the curricular process ... in which teacher, learners, subject matter and milieu are in dynamic interaction. (p. 392)

Similar to Hampton's (1995) and Mary's earlier noted thoughts about Aboriginal education, Clandinin and Connelly's (1992; Connelly & Clandinin, 1988) calls for understanding curriculum as a life in the making drew attention to the need for understanding the deeply narrative, experiential aspects at work in the meeting of "teachers' and children's lives together in schools and classrooms" (p. 392). By focusing attention on these narrative experiential aspects of curriculum making, Clandinin and Connelly highlighted the negotiated, relational nature of curriculum making. In time, Janice, with Karen Keats Whelan and Clandinin, noted that central within these relational negotiations within curriculum making were children's and teacher's identity making, an understanding which creates a sense of urgency for the co-creation of "classroom spaces where teachers might narratively engage with children about who they are and who they are becoming" (Huber, Keats Whelan, & Clandinin, 2003a, p. 303).

Collectively, we carried calls of the need for attending to curriculum making as a negotiated, relational, life making process shaped in the meeting of diverse lives. Curriculum making is an unfolding process in which identities are shaped and reshaped. As we attended to the experiences of Jennifer, Jerri-Lynn, Khea, Lucy, Lulu, and Brenda Mary as they navigated post-secondary places we tried to stay wakeful to their lived and told stories of their experiences in diverse situations, both in and outside of post-secondary places. We were also attentive to the tensions they experienced as their lives came into conflict with dominant institutional narratives which prescribe the knowledge, ways of knowing, and of representing knowledge currently privileged in most post-secondary places.

1.2.3. Identity

After years of inquiry alongside teachers, Connelly and Clandinin (1999) conceptualized "stories to live by" as a narrative way to understand the connections among teachers' knowledge, contexts, and identities. This narrative way of understanding identity has shaped narrative inquiries focusing on teachers' and administrators' identities (Huber & Whelan, 2000; Nelson, 2003; Steeves, 2000; Whelan & Huber, 2000); narrative inquiries into children's and teachers' identity making and curriculum making (Clandinin et al., 2006; Hong, 2009; Huber & Clandinin, 2005; Murphy, 2004; Pearce, 2005); narrative inquiries into children's, families, and teacher's identity making and curriculum making (Chung, 2008; Clandinin, Murphy, & Huber, 2011; Huber, 2008; Huber, Clandinin, & Murphy, 2011; Zhao, 2007); narrative inquiry into language as identity in the lives of Aboriginal post-secondary students (Young, 2003, 2005b); and narrative inquiry into the lives of Chinese international students in Canadian post-secondary contexts (Li, 2006).

As, for example, Clandinin and Huber (2002) inquired into the stories of Darlene, a mother of *Inuit* ancestry with whom they and Keats Whelan engaged in narrative inquiry in a city center school in western Canada, they wrote that in understanding identity as stories to live by we need to understand

> identity is a storied life composition, a story to live by. Stories to live by are shaped in places and lived in places. They live in actions, in relationships with others, in language, including silences, in gaps and vacancies, in continuities and discontinuities. (pp. 161–162)

As Mary, too, worked with this narrative understanding of identity as stories to live by as a way to understand the identities of the Aboriginal post-secondary students with whom she engaged in narrative inquiry during her doctoral research, she wrote that this narrative understanding of identity

> felt congruent with who I am, have become and continue to become. It felt congruent with what I wanted to study, which was language as identity. Through my proposal, I began telling my story and, as I relived significant moments in my life, I came to recognize and understand that narrative inquiry honours how Aboriginal people learn and gain knowledge. (2003, p. 30)

For Greg Cajete (2001), too, there are indelible connections between story and identity. He writes that:

> Telling the story of one's journey is tracing one's steps through people, events and places that formed you. And as we pause at each special memory we realize that we have indeed been formed by our encounters with the stories of others. (p. 9)

Collectively, we carried calls of the need for understanding stories to live by as we attended to the experiences of Jerri-Lynn, Khea, Lucy, Lulu, Brenda Mary, and Jennifer as they navigated post-secondary places. In doing so, we tried to stay wakeful to their lived and told stories as they negotiated their identities alongside Aboriginal and non-Aboriginal students and faculty and post-secondary places often shaped by policies, processes, curriculum, and knowledge significantly different from their own.

1.2.4. Place

The places where Aboriginal children and youth have learned to live and tell their stories is of particular significance and is often not attended to in the curriculum making and identity making they experience in public school classrooms. As described earlier, it is equally unlikely that Aboriginal post-secondary students find spaces to attend to the significance of place in their learning and becoming. School and university classrooms often do not typically offer, nor seek to honour or shape, the kind of wisdom of which Keith Basso (1996) describes as he writes of what the *Apache* horseman, Dudley Patterson, taught him about learning shaped through careful attention to place, relationship, and story:

> Wisdom sits in places. It's like water that never dries up. You need to drink water to stay alive, don't you? Well, you also need to drink from places. You must remember everything about them. You must learn their names. You must remember what happened at them long ago. You must think about it and keep on thinking about it. Then ... you will be wise. (p. 127)

This idea of "wisdom sit[ting] in places" draws attention to the history of a place, to a deep felt understanding that our ancestors have been there before us. The places where we live are the places where stories have already been lived and told that shaped the place, the stories that live there, the kind of structures that shape the place. For example, residential schools are places that have shaped the lived and told stories of Aboriginal students through "intergenerational narrative reverberations" which Mary names as the stories "we all carry in our bodies, in our memories, in our souls" (2005b, p. 162). As she draws on Mary Catherine Bateson's (2000) thinking that we have each "been shaped by [our] individual history and the histories of our communities" (p. 227), Mary describes that the stories we live and tell show the interactions, the relational connections, between and across generations. Understanding these indelible connections in the stories to live by, in the lives of Aboriginal post-secondary students shapes an urgency to attend to the intergenerational narrative reverberations of residential schools in each student's lived and told stories. However, this is not enough. Residential schools adopted the practices and curricular structures of other Eurocentric schools, practices, and curricular structures that continue to shape schools and post-secondary places where, today, Aboriginal students attend. It is impossible to imagine understanding the experiences of Aboriginal students without attending to the place of school with the understandings of residential schools from the vantage point of Aboriginal peoples. Such understandings of place raise questions about the sense of belonging, alienation, and isolation Aboriginal students may experience in post-secondary places.

Collectively, we carried calls of the need to stay wakeful to place(s) as we attended to the experiences of Khea, Lucy, Lulu, Brenda Mary, Jennifer, and Jerri-Lynn as they navigated post-secondary places. In doing so, we tried to stay wakeful to ways in which a place or places shaped their stories to live by as teachers.

Our shared concerns about past and current realities facing Aboriginal post-secondary students, teachers, children, youth, families, Elders, and communities brought us, this circle of women already mentioned, as well as two Elders, Sister Dorothy Moore and Florence Paynter, into sustained relationships as we co-inquired into the experiences of Aboriginal post-secondary students becoming teachers in post-secondary places. The title for this chapter, "Not Tomorrow ... Today" emerged in the midst of our relational narrative inquiry. In our third whole group gathering in Winnipeg, as the storied lives shared in our circle became increasingly focused upon the urgent, yet slow, change happening in relation with high school and post-secondary completion of Aboriginal students in Canada, Mary and Janice recounted their reading of Monty Pryor's (1998) story about his Aunty Pauline who, when he asked her to share stories of her life with him, said:

> "You know, I can tell you fellus lotta deadly stories. I can sing you lotta deadly songs and do lotta deadly dancin'. I could write you a deadly book too." She stopped, waved her arms in the air and shrugged her shoulders, then said, "Nah! Maybe tomorrow. Maybe tomorrow." (p. 120)

Thinking with Aunty Pauline's story deepened our recognition of the urgency of our sharing of our storied lives, today, instead of waiting until tomorrow. We are hopeful that as readers engage with our lived and told stories of our lives we might have a place in shaping a more equitable and just, a more hope-filled future for next generations of Aboriginal post-secondary students and teachers.

1.3. OUR HOPES FOR OUR BOOK

The long-term relational narrative inquiry from which this book emerged was, all along, a work-in-progress. We did not start this shared inquiry by imagining that we would co-author this book. However, as we gathered, collectively sharing and inquiring into stories of our lives, the idea of a book started to wind into and across our conversations. Soon, this idea of co-making a book became an aspect of many of our conversations, as did our hopes for what it might open up and change for Aboriginal students as they navigate post-secondary places in becoming teachers.

Through our inquiry into our storied lives we are hopeful that diverse audiences will find meaning and support. Given our central inquiry focus which was to understand the experiences of Lucy, Lulu, Brenda Mary, Jennifer, Jerri-Lynn, and Khea as they navigated post-secondary places in becoming teachers, we hope Aboriginal students, wherever they are composing their lives, will find support in our stories, support to stay on their journeys of becoming teachers. As noted earlier, given the increasing population of Aboriginal children and youth in Canada, their presence in Canadian schools, in Aboriginal or rural or urban schools is vital. We need you, Aboriginal teachers and non-Aboriginal teachers, as our colleagues, as warriors alongside us.

Inquiring into our storied lives supports us to show readers crucial ways in which our families, parents, grandparents, Elders, partners, siblings, children, communities, and community members sustain our becoming teachers, past and present. As our stories show, although we each face complexities as we are composing our lives these sustaining relationships keep us moving toward our dreams. In contrast to the stereotypical narratives often shaped and told through the media or by government officials, and also at times by people in professions with intentions to provide care or support for us, our familial relationships, as Aboriginal people and women, have been honouring. Given what we know of the strength of Aboriginal families we hope that as parents, grandparents, partners, siblings, or children of Aboriginal post-secondary students read this book they will feel, hear, and see reflections of themselves, reflections of their importance in the education of Aboriginal and non-Aboriginal children, youth, and post-secondary students, past, present, and future.

We hope, too, that people who work with agencies, both government and community-based, who provide funding for the post-secondary education of Aboriginal students will learn new ways of supporting us. Because many of us needed to live away from our communities and families while we studied to become teachers, we faced many emotional and financial burdens. We also, at times, were deeply harmed by the myths many non-Aboriginal people held of the funding received by Aboriginal communities for post-secondary education. Our storied lives are a testimony to the fact that post-secondary funding for Aboriginal students in Canada is shameful. We hope that as Aboriginal and non-Aboriginal people read this book they will join us in demanding necessary and respectful funding for post-secondary education.

Five of us were or became practicing teachers during the years of our relational narrative inquiry. While many times we felt supported by our school board directors as we navigated our professional contexts as Aboriginal teachers, sometimes we did not. We hope that as school board directors come to know our storied lives they might realize new relationships with Aboriginal teachers, present and current, in their boards. Spaces shaped with openness were crucial for us to name who we each were becoming as Aboriginal people and teachers. There is rich diversity among us and we need school board directors to recognize, and value, both these differences and strengths.

As our relational narrative inquiry into our storied lives shows, teacher educators *can* hold a critical place in our becoming Aboriginal teachers. Alongside teacher educators we can find spaces where all of who we are, in all of our diversity and complexity, is valued. In these kinds of relationships in teacher education we can feel safe to learn as we know we can trust both how and what we learn because who we are has not been denied, shamed, silenced, or made invisible. We hope that as teacher educators read our book they will pay attention to the feelings of resonance *and* dissonance you experience in relation with our storied lives. Particularly as teacher educators feel dissonance with our storied lives, we urge them to inquire into their stories to live by. We hope that in this way, through their own inquiries into their storied lives alongside our storied lives, the experiences of present and future generations of Aboriginal students in teacher education programs might support their becoming, in diverse ways and in all of their multiplicities and differences.

Rita Joe, a world renowned *Mi'kmaq* poet, reminds us that "we need to teach well so that others will know about us" (2000, p. 52). We hope that we have done this, that through storying and restorying our lives in this book that our relational narrative inquiry shows and teaches well both the complexities and possibilities experienced by Lucy, Lulu, Brenda Mary, Jennifer, Jerri-Lynn, and Khea as we navigated post-secondary places in becoming teachers. Many lives, present and future, depend upon our teaching well so that others may see their responsibilities and in doing so, choose to become warriors alongside us in a more than 500-year struggle for equity and justice for Aboriginal people in Canada.

NOTES

1. Learning from Linda Tuhiwai Smith (1999), we italicize *naayapikang* as a way to respect the *Anishinabe* language and to honour all people of the *Anishinabe* nation. Throughout our book we italicize the names of each nation and all Aboriginal languages.

2. We use the term Aboriginal to include First Nations, *Metís*, and *Inuit*.

CHAPTER 2

INTRODUCING OURSELVES: STORIED EXPERIENCES SHAPING THE STORIES WE LIVE BY

Writing, much like composing a life (Bateson, 1989), is not a straightforward, linear process. Indeed, storying and restorying lives is, as highlighted in the writing of Marmon Silko (1996), a winding, crisscrossing process:

> For those of you accustomed to being taken from point A to point B to point C, this presentation may be somewhat difficult to follow. Pueblo expression resembles something like a spider's web – with many little threads radiating from the centre, crisscrossing one another. As with the web, the structure emerges as it is made, and you must simply listen and trust, as the Pueblo people do, that meaning will be made. (pp. 48–49)

As we shared and inquired into our storied lives in narrative inquiry circles in Manitoba and Nova Scotia, and then again in yearly whole group narrative inquiry circles, we grew in our knowing of one another, of one another's lives, of where we are each from, of one another's stories to live by. In Chapter 1, we gave a sense of some of the places from which Mary and Janice are from and of ways in which their experiences in these places drew them toward ideas which they began to thread together as a way to shape a frame for our relational narrative inquiry. In this chapter we invite readers to gain a sense of the multiplicity of people, and the multiplicity of lives which shaped our relational narrative inquiry.

Storied Experiences Shaping Brenda Mary's Life

Aaniin Boozhoo
I need to heal from the loss of language
The way I am doing that is by learning it

I will tell you a story about my father
He attended Elkhorn School
This is the same place Percy Bird attended
I do not know if he knew my dad
My dad was young
When they relocated from the original site of Chief Peguis the people were known
    then by Saint Peters Reserve
My dad was born around 1910
He never really knew his birthday
It was never formally recorded for him
When he grew old
The Canadian government told him by mail he could pick his birthday
He started receiving old age pension
He chose *Manoominike giizis niishtana shi niiwin*, August 24
When he died he was *niizhwaaso midina she niswi*

When he went away to boarding school
He was a child
He had wishes like any other child
He wished for sweets, candy, gum, and other kind of sweet treats
He and another child at the school made up a song about candy, gum, and sweet
    treats
It went like this:
"You give me some
I give you some when my mother comes on Sunday"
They used to wish for other children's goodies when they had them and promised
    if they were given some they would give some back when their mothers
    came on Sunday

But
My dad's mother died before he went to school
He never had a mother's nurturing
The way I did
Because his mother died when he was young he was raised at the boarding school
He drank a lot as he got older
And he would sing that song
And my older sister too
They also attended boarding school
And they too sang that song
It is a sad song
It makes me feel sad for the people when they were small and young and needed a
    mother's love
And the kind of love that is shared in families
My dad never had that
He did his best as a father for his children
There were 12 of us
He never wanted us to go away to boarding school

However
Some of my older brothers and sister did go
They went to Dauphin, McKay Residential School, Birtle, and Teulon
They suffered losses in these places
No one likes to talk about it much
Even my dad never really talked about it
He just sang that sad little song

When I think about that song
It makes me feel sad for my dad
I picture him as the little child who wanted goodies and love and the warm
    feelings you get inside
From being nurtured

He grew up
He met my mother
Fell in love with her
Married her
Together they had 12 children
All but one grew up and we each have families of our own
We are a close family
We love one another
We continue to be a large family
My father went on to care for our community
He served as band councillor for a couple of terms in the year I was born
He worked in the area of education
To bring schools to the reserve so that little children did not have to leave their
    families and their homes to attend school away from home and family
I felt proud of my dad when I learned he was a band councillor for the people
He was a leader and outspoken
He spoke up for the people
He helped in any way he could
The old people who are still alive today remember my dad in that way
There was no welfare then
So he would walk around going from house to house
Checking on the peoples' well being
If they needed anything like food such as flour or baking powder
He would help them
The people liked that
They liked it when he would speak up for them
They even wanted him to be the Chief
In a way I guess he was the Chief, the leader

I need to say something here about today's generation
They don't know things like this about my dad
Who he was before he became old
He broke the trail for people who are today's leaders by speaking up for
    education and to have these schools on our reserve

There used to be three schools
One in the centre where we lived
One in the south
One in the north
The reserve is big
The reserve needed three schools because children used to walk to school
Now children are bussed to one school from K-12
Someday
I want to see and hear my father receive credit or acknowledgement for what he
    did as a leader in our community
Sometime soon, before all the old people who remembered him in these ways
    die with their memories of him
They are the ones who told me things about my dad
Even though he suffered
Both when he lived in the residential school
Then for the remainder of his life
From the effects of living there
He used those experiences to make things better for the people
Once he was given the opportunity to do that

Miigwetch
I needed to say that for my dad
Myself and my family
And my children
And grandchildren
And great grandchildren
And the *Anishinabe* people of Peguis
The rest of Manitoba
Canada
All the Indigenous people who are and were affected by colonialism
We have it within our power
Now
To shape our own destiny
(Word image composed from Brenda Mary's journal entry written on October 13, 2007)

Storied Experiences Shaping Sister Dorothy's Life

I'm a retired educator
Still very involved in education
It is here
In this community of Membertou
That I was born and began my educational journey
And
It is here that I've returned to be an educational consultant for my community
Yes, I've come full circle
And within this circle are experiences I went through to obtain an education when
    no one believed I was capable of achieving anything resembling academic
    success

The residential school labeled me
As "stupid"
And a "jackass"
The middle grade teachers in the public school sent me home to the "backwoods
    where I belonged"

The high school was reluctant to permit me to write the provincial exams because
    I was considered a potential failure
Yet
Despite it all
My determination to acquire what was not generally available to "Indians"
Finally became a reality
But not without its scars
Mostly because of racism
Discrimination
Prejudice
And
Being considered as "less than"
Associated with being Aboriginal

For many years
I have been involved in providing education
To hundreds of children and young adults
In schools and universities
Ever keeping in mind the importance of being respectful
To every individual
In the belief
That each is in a process of becoming all they are meant to be and can be

Yes
Everything we experience along life's journey plays a vital part in forming and
    fashioning our lives
I was born 76 years ago
Right here on the reservation where I currently work
My childhood home on this reservation is still there
I started my educational journey in a one-room school
I also went to a residential school
Although I am officially retired
I currently work as an educational consultant for our Band
I am also on the road a lot serving on many different boards and committees

A passion that has been part of my life for many years is to help others
Even if it's only one person at a time
To understand who we are as *Mi'kmaq* people
My hope is that through an increased understanding of Aboriginal peoples non-
    Aboriginal peoples might change some of their attitudes toward us

Another passion in my work in education for the province and with our Band is to
    keep asking the question:
What can I do to make our curriculum more inclusive for *Mi'kmaq* learners and
    for non-*Mi'kmaq* learners?
For a few years of my life
I worked at the local university
It wasn't always easy
Especially in the beginning
I remember this one sociology professor saying something to me about the
    "Indian table"
I said, "What do you mean by 'Indian table'?"
He said, "The table where all the Indian students sit."
I said, "How can you label it the Indian table? It can't be an Indian table when
    it's made out of wood. Besides, why don't you call that table over
    there the Bayside table; the table over there the Coalminer's table; that
    one the Uplands table?"
I was shocked because he was a sociologist
Yet, he seemed to be so racist

Through my life I have learned
That the racism
The colonization
Is not going to go away tomorrow or next year
But, we can't stop fighting
We have to keep on fighting

I never want to stop what I am doing
Over my lifetime
I have faced serious illnesses
Each time I've risen again
Each time I've been able to get up and to go at it again
I do what I can
Each day
There is so much to be done
(Word image composed from Sister Dorothy's experiences storied in narrative inquiry
circles on November, 2005; January, 2006; & May, 2010)

Storied Experiences Shaping Florence's Life

I learned
Each [of my grandchildren]
Is unique
With their own needs
Own strengths
And definitely
Their own character

Today
My time was spent chauffeuring my daughter
To meet my granddaughter at the Manitoba Youth Centre
My daughter had scheduled a visit with her daughter
It is a timed visit of 45 minutes
We arrived at 1:10 and we went in
I saw a woman who was also there visiting her granddaughter
We greeted one another
Something she said struck a chord with me
She commented on how we seem to meet one another
All the time
All over the place
If it's not in a place like this visiting granddaughters
It is in helping other people
Who are dealing with their own residential school experiences and dealing with
    trauma
Other times
It's facing our own family challenges
Trying to make everything functional
For all of us

I know that as a mother
I tried to raise my children in the best way I could
I know my daughter is doing the same
Yet, somehow, here we are
Visiting a child
Who has been affected by the ongoing impact of colonization on our people
When will this sense of helplessness end for us?

We are in the waiting area
When my granddaughter arrives
Her mom and one of her sisters rushes to greet her
I continue to wait by the chairs
My granddaughter spots me
She comes rushing toward me and begins to sob
We hug and hold one another for a long time and then we kiss
We are all so happy to see her

Once a week
For the next two months
We will get a chance to come for a visit with her and a sense of hope
That it will all get better
We can never give up hope
And especially for one another
Word image composed from Florence's journal entries written in December, 2007 & on
August 28, 2010)

Storied Experiences Shaping Jennifer's Life

I was just offered a permanent contract
With a Winnipeg school division
I am ecstatic
But
Have no one to share my excitement with

My fiancé
Is not answering his phone
My parents are not home
And my classmates at the University
Are so focused on their experiences
That I feel
My news
Would make them feel sad
About not getting offered a job

I don't want to put
That kind of pressure
On them
I know
They would be happy for me
But
I can't help but worry
That they might think
This offer is unfair
There has been some bitterness expressed toward the idea of individuals of
        minority backgrounds
Being given preference
Over others
Who are Caucasian

This situation creates a bit of a stigma
That I was hired because I am an Aboriginal person
I am an Aboriginal person
I can agree that this may have been a characteristic
Upon which their decision was based
But
I believe that I've worked hard to get where I am
I believe I was offered the job based
On my impression made on the interviewers
And that I am a capable person
Who will be an excellent teacher

So, why is it 2 hours later
And I haven't shared this news with anybody?

I suppose I asked this question
Because I was searching
For the reason
As though the universe
Is always trying to tell us
Something
Why I was alone
In these hours
Following this great announcement
Perhaps
I felt guilt
For being seen as advantaged
And slighted
By the notion
That I may
Have been hired
Just because
I am Aboriginal

This attitude
Also holds
For Aboriginal hires

If this was the reason
Then
Maybe
I needed the time
To get over this belief
Before
I could
Truly celebrate
This gift
Accomplishment
With others

Whatever the reason
I now believe
That I was
One of the best candidates
For teaching
That any division
Had to choose from
I would like to add
That shortly after
I wrote the earlier entry
Another school division
Called me

To offer
Me
A permanent contract
I am currently completing
The last 2 weeks of teaching
In my first year
(Word image composed from Jennifer's journal entries written on February, 2006 &
June, 2007)

Storied Experiences Shaping Jerri-Lynn's Life

I was very encouraged
What Mary shared with me
She said to not let anyone burn out the fire within me
No one can put out the fire except you

A guy who's also Aboriginal
Said that he couldn't believe I was "native"
I know it shouldn't bother me
But
I just can't help it
It really did affect me more than I thought
I had never really thought about my "nativeness"
Until I started university
Really
It didn't start until I walked into the Aboriginal Centre
For the first time
To figure out if I was really smart enough
To go to university

That was really when I embraced who I thought I was
A little bit of white
And a little bit of native
I love that I have *Cree*
In my family
I love the culture
And the language
I love the people

But
Is there a way to be Aboriginal
Or is it who you are
Inside?

Silly question
But
Some may say it is how you act
Some say it is who you are

Just some thoughts

It is true that I felt a little bit weird
Going to the Aboriginal Centre
After
I thought about what that man said to me
I thought what if everybody there sees me that way

I know it is just my own insecurities
And I will just have to get over them

I am so torn whether I should even try and use my *Cree*
Teaching it I mean
I don't want to be looked at as the white chick trying to be Aboriginal
LOL

I laugh because as I reread that statement
It sounds so funny
I am not a fluent speaker
But would love to be

I don't think I am good enough
To teach it though

My thoughts are so complicated
Trying to get out
Exactly
What I am trying to say

Stan
My husband
Has been my rock
Even though we have had some bumpy roads
He has been one of my biggest supporters
When my mom passed away
He knew what I was going through
He lost his mom at a young age
He walked through with me
Every bit of pain I felt
He held my hand and helped carry me through
It was then that I fell in love with him
All over again
He helped shape me to become strong
To live through such a hard experience
To keep on keeping on
(Word image composed from Jerri-Lynn's journal entries written in
December, 2007 & on August 28, 2010)

Storied Experiences Shaping Khea's Life

I think it is important in our graduate classes
We need to keep coming back
To the ongoing impact of colonization on our people

At the end of one of my graduate courses
Another student of *Mi'kmaq* ancestry and I
Did our presentation in *Mi'kmaq*
And we modelled the residential school
Some of the students were almost crying
We started our presentation by handing out a reading in the *Mi'kmaq* language
    to the class
Then Joan (pseudonym) said in *Mi'kmaq*,
"Okay, now we're going to read through this"
All of the students who were not *Mi'kmaq*
Were all looking
I was the only other person in the room who understood *Mi'kmaq*
So I stood up and acted like I was the teacher's pet
Joan was almost yelling at the other student
She kept saying
"*Elsapet*" (which means "Elizabeth" in *Mi'kmaq*)
The other student was trying to figure out
What Joan was saying
She finally figured out that Joan was telling her to read the text
The student turned red and she started to try to read
But her pronunciations were funny

I was pretending to laugh
And then Joan and I
Speaking in *Mi'kmaq* with each other
Pretended to make fun of the student

This was like what happened
To children
Who were *Mi'kmaq* speakers
When they went to residential school
This still happens
To *Mi'kmaq* children today when they are forced to speak English in front of their
    classmates

Well the student
Who is an adult
And who had agreed to do the role play with us
Her eyes even watered
It was like she was ready to cry

We said, "Okay, that's enough"
You could see the stress in the classroom

"*Elsapet*" said she felt alienated and now understood what *Mi'kmaq* students
Must have felt
And still feel

The body language
And postures
Of the non-*Mi'kmaq* students
Changed
(Word image composed from Khea's experiences storied in a narrative inquiry circle in
December, 2007)

Storied Experiences Shaping Lucy's Life

I remember that as a child
I was a Grade 2 student attending the nearby public school
It was close to lunch
At the time we went home to eat
I remember feeling tired and hungry
The teacher instructed me to finish two pages of hand writing
When I was done I would get free time
As I was doing my assigned work the other students were finishing their work
    before me
I wanted free time too
I began to rush
My handwriting became messy
I was finally finished and placed my book on the bottom of the pile located on the
    table at the back of the classroom
I was relieved to have finished and happy to finally have free time
About 5 minutes into free time the teacher called me up to her desk
I was standing next to her desk when she pulled my hand writing book up into the
    air
She asked me, "What is this?"
I did not respond
So she asked me again, but in a much louder voice
I still did not answer
What happened next is a memory I blocked out for many years
The teacher took me by the hand and walked me to the chalk board
She then asked me to show the class my work
I felt frightened and just stood there with her at the chalk board
The teacher then grabbed me by the hand and guided it to the chalk board
The teacher forced my hand to make scribble marks on the board
I just stood there staring at the board
She
On the other hand
Screamed that I was "nothing but a dirty black Indian"
Tears began to fall down my cheeks
I remember the students staring at me
In complete silence

Then
A teacher from the next classroom came in
She took me by my hand and guided me into her class
It was there I stayed until lunch

As an adult
And as an educator
I think leadership is another place where we continue to follow ways forced
        onto us that are not *Mi'kmaq* ways
What I'm thinking about is that we need to widen what we mean by leadership
Not as something done by one person
But by everyone
A child could be a leader
A parent could be a leader
A teaching assistant could be a leader

I think
As teachers
And administrators
In First Nations schools
We have to stop saying
"I did that"
Or
"I brought that in"
We need to move away from "I" to "we"

Who cares who started something?
What matters most
Is how the idea became embraced by everyone
And that it supports
Children
In their learning

We need to stop claiming an idea
Or competing to have the best idea

Instead
We need to share our ideas

We can never work well as a team
If we keep saying
I
I
I

I am trying to raise this with the principal
Of my school

And
Also
The people who govern education in our community
When I make suggestions that I think would move us from I to we
I keep hearing
"No"
Sometimes I try to say more
Even when I hear
"No"
But
Sometimes I get afraid of losing my job
People have lost their jobs for not doing
Exactly
What they are told to do

With our people
It used to be that we listened to all voices
To the voices of people of all ages
As decisions were made
We need to get back to this
Right now this seems unheard of in our schools
(Word image composed from Lucy's experiences storied in a narrative inquiry circle in
February, 2008)

Storied Experiences Shaping Lulu's Life

I became a teacher because when I was in Grade 9
I had started Grade 9 at our local school
I went to the Director of Education
To ask for a *Mi'kmaq* language speaker to teach me—in my language
Not once did he tell me there wasn't a *Mi'kmaq* language teacher
Therefore, I went off reserve with a friend
We went to the White school because they spoke or would teach me in English
   language anyway
After Christmas break
I wasn't allowed to go to the White school because of road conditions
I was 13 years old
When I returned to the local school in January I was looked at like
"Hum, what is she doing here?"
But being an eager learner I didn't care
When graduation came in June
The Grade 9 graduating class got to go to Manitoba for a trip
I wasn't allowed to go because I hadn't been at the school the whole year
I was being punished
But I didn't care

When I decided to become a teacher
I knew I wanted to teach the language
Almost 30 years have passed when I was in Grade 9

But today
There are only a very few people who do know and speak the language
That's why I wanted to become a teacher
I do not want students to be punished because of the language
My mission and philosophy today
Inside and outside of school
Is to teach the language
And to always let students know to speak the language around me
Never would I ever punish students
Physically and emotionally
For not speaking the language
They know to speak it
If I don't remind the students, who will?
That's what I believe in
To allow students to express themselves in the language
(Word image composed from Lulu's stories shared in a narrative inquiry circle in
August, 2010)

CHAPTER 3

CO-COMPOSING RELATIONAL NARRATIVE INQUIRY

Beginnings in Mary's Lived Experience

Throughout my educational journey
In anthropology and sociology
I wondered about research
I was genuinely interested in research
On Aboriginal people
But I realized
Research was rarely undertaken
With Aboriginal people
I wondered
About the purpose of the research
About who would benefit from the research
It seemed like anthropologists
Drove
Or flew into our communities
Did their work
And left
Never to be heard from again

I felt
It appeared
As though the researchers
Knew more about us
Than we did ourselves
How we viewed ourselves as *Anishinabe*
Was not public knowledge
However
The ways we were perceived or understood by researchers
Was the knowledge
Taught and readily disseminated in the classroom

Early
In my educational journey
First in high school
And more so in university
I felt
Uncomfortable
With the research on Aboriginal people
What the research portrayed
Was rarely positive
None of the researchers
Were of Aboriginal ancestry
If Aboriginal people
Were involved
They were merely
"Informants"
Never
Co-researchers
We did not
Have a voice
(Word image composed from Mary's written story shared in fall, 2005)

Beginnings in Janice's Lived Experience

I started a master's program
With questions of children's lives in classrooms
I was carrying many tensions
With dominant stories of school
Stories that
In school
Knowledge was separated into "subject matters"
And, too
That all of the complex
Shifting and rich knowing of children
Could be measured through standardized achievement tests

As I began I knew little about research
But, in time I realized that at the heart of my interest
Was understanding experience through story

In a course with Jean Clandinin
I was encouraged to write and to inquire into stories of my experience
In this way the focus of my thesis research emerged
I wanted to return to an elementary classroom
To engage in collaborative narrative inquiry
With a teacher and children
But, on the broader university landscape
I was often told
Warned

That narrative research was not considered rigorous
That collaborative inquiry was not valued in academia
I faced many questions about how to determine
If the stories children told were true
This response left me feeling
Disillusioned and ignorant
It seemed as though my questions and passions as a teacher
Were naïve and silly
And were certainly not of any value
In the "real" research world
(Word image composed from Janice's written story shared in fall, 2005)

When Mary and Janice first met they were doctoral students, each carrying multiple and differing experiences. In time, as they participated in a weekly research issues seminar at the Centre for Research for Teacher Education and Development at the University of Alberta, they came to know a post-secondary place where, as described by Trihn Minh-ha (1989), the unwinding threads of their storied lives, including stories such as the two earlier stories, could be voiced and were seen as worthy of serious attention and respect. As a post-secondary place, research issues was/is attended by graduate students, resident and visiting faculty, as well as members of the broader community. In this ongoing meeting of diverse lives spaces were shaped where people shared thoughts about, and inquired into, complexities and possibilities of composing identities as researchers (Steeves, 2004). Because the research issues table was/is a place open to everyone,

No one knows ahead of time who will join the table or what the conversation will bring forward. Instead, each research issues conversation evolves in unique ways because agendas are not prescribed but rather are drawn naturally from individual people's lives and research puzzles. While participants bring a range of research puzzles and methodologies to the conversation, each person is invited to share her [or his] inquiries in conversation. As this conversational inquiry moves gently around the table one [person] to another, participants come to know the necessity of creating a safe and caring tone for sharing work and experiences in their lives, for inquiring and voicing concerns related to issues of research and teacher education. (Steeves et al., 2009, p. 308)

This focus on attending to and puzzling over lives in the making shaped Janice and Mary's relationship; it also drew each of them toward the potential for change as shaped through the deeply relational aspects of narrative inquiry as a research methodology.

As Janice and Mary were coming to know one another at the research issues table and in a subsequent course with Jean on narrative inquiry, Janice had been teaching in rural, international, and city center schools and Mary had worked for many years in a post-secondary institution. In their sharing with one another stories of these experiences, a relationship began to take shape where, in trust, the hard and often tension-filled and uneasy stories of their experiences were shared; stories like the following:

Mary

I am reminded of my experiences in Pine Creek Residential School
When I was not allowed to speak *Anishinabemowin*
Or the other students and I would be punished
At the age of 14 I did not see this substitution as brainwashing
Today
As I read more
And teach
About the purposes of the residential school system
I have come to understand that it was brainwashing to keep me insulated from my
    parents
From our *Anishinabe* culture, values, and beliefs
I was offered
A substitute
And this is now one of the "stories I live by" (Connelly & Clandinin, 1999, p. 4)

When I began my educational journey
In my masters program
A feat very few Aboriginal students engaged in
I did not know what "thesis" or "research" meant
At that time
Aboriginal students were not in graduate programs
We were not encouraged to pursue such an endeavour
This lack of encouragement made us feel as though
We were deemed as incapable
As the former Director of Aboriginal Student Services
And currently
As a faculty member in the Faculty of Education
Encouraging Aboriginal students
To dream about going to graduate school
Is a responsibility
I love taking seriously
Aboriginal people
Belong in universities
Aboriginal people
Are or can become
Excellent researchers

As *Anishinabe kwe*
I have come to understand the importance of knowing who we are and where we
    come from
According to the Royal Commission on Aboriginal People (1996)
"Education is seen as the vehicle for both enhancing the life of the individual and
    reaching collective goals" (p. 433)

As well
"Consistent with Aboriginal traditions education must develop the whole child
Intellectually, spiritually, emotionally and physically" (p. 434)
However
"Rather than nurturing the individual
Schooling experiences typically erode
Identity and self-worth" (p. 434)
The commission concluded that
The "destiny of a people
Is intricately bound
To the ways
Its children
Are educated
Education
Is the transmission
Of cultural DNA
From one generation
To the next
It shapes the language
And pathways of thinking
The contours of character
And values
The social skills
And creative potential
Of the individual
It determines
The productive skills
Of a people" (p. 433)

As an Aboriginal educator
This makes me understand the impact of the residential school system and how it eroded
Many of these traditions, values, and beliefs

My wonder
At this point
Is how this may continue to impact
Aboriginal students
Who are now in post-secondary education
I have come to understand that if we
As Aboriginal and non-Aboriginal educators
Want to understand
And acknowledge
The experiences of Aboriginal students in university
We need to acknowledge and understand
The development
And purposes
Of the residential school system in Canada
If we are unable to do that

The education of Aboriginal people in Canada
Remains a void
A void we no longer can ignore
(Word image composed from Mary's reflections written in summer, 2004)

In storying her experiences Mary highlighted that the legacy of the residential schools in Canada is still relevant in present times because it continues to shape the lives of Aboriginal people today. As Hampton (1995) suggested "brainwashing" occurs "when education is used to wipe out identity, language, culture, philosophy, and substitute something else for these" (p. 52). While Mary knows this process from within her own life and schooling experiences, it is a process Janice slowly awakened to as an elementary teacher alongside children and families of Aboriginal ancestry:

Janice

Even today
I feel sick when I think about it
When I remember
Ryley's (pseudonym) face
And his words
That Tuesday morning
In the fall of 2000
When he entered our Grade 5 classroom and exclaimed
"What happened to our classroom? All of our stuff is gone!"
Ryley was referring to all of the books, experience centres, and materials
Kites, rugs, book shelves, music, pillows, and plants
That no longer shaped the physical space
Of our classroom
He was right
Everything
Except the old graffiti scratched desks
There when we arrived in August
Was gone

Ryley
Was a young boy of *Cree* ancestry
Whom I first met in a city centre school in a large western Canadian city
The year we met
Ryley was in Grade 3
During his Grade 4 year
Ryley's teacher, Karen
Children in the classroom and four mothers
Were co-researchers with Jean and me
In a narrative inquiry attending to the meeting of the diverse lives of children,
        families, teachers, and administrators

In Canadian schools[1]
Over the year of the inquiry
Close relationships developed
Including close relationships
With Ryley and his mom, Sylvia
During the year we learned that
As part of a new partnership the next school year
Karen, Jean, and I
Along with a number of friends
Were moving to another school in the city centre
When Ryley and Sylvia heard this news
They talked often about wanting to be there
As school started in the fall of 2000
Ryley was there
In the Grade 5 classroom
Over the summer he, Sylvia, and their family
Moved homes so that Ryley could attend school there
As a way to continue to engage in relational narrative inquiry with Ryley and
    Sylvia
And with other Aboriginal children and families
We applied for and received funding for a grant focused on reshaping classrooms
    and schools
By learning from the stories of Aboriginal children and families[2]

However
As my beginning shows
Our time together with Ryley and Sylvia and the other children and families
At the new school
Was short-lived
Tensions
About the disrespect toward Aboriginal children and families
In the school
Which began to emerge through our work on the grant
Became so intense that the 10-year vision for the new partnership
Quickly dissolved
This meant that staff
Such as myself
Whose positioning in the school was connected with the university
Needed to leave the school

The following summer I moved across the country and began teaching in the
    School of Education at St. Francis Xavier University
In B. Ed. courses
I soon began meeting students of *Mi'kmaq* ancestry
People whose stories of their earlier experiences in public schools
Resonated
With the stories Ryley and Sylvia, and much earlier, which Mary shared with me
In my knowing of these stories

I felt responsible to seek change
(Word image composed from Janice's reflections written in fall, 2005)

In the space shaped in the meeting of these and other stories, Janice and Mary were drawn toward many questions about the educational experiences of children, youth, families, and adults of Aboriginal ancestry in Canadian schools and universities. Their storied experiences and subsequent questions shaped the emergence of this relational narrative inquiry which, as earlier described, focused on understanding the experiences of Brenda Mary, Jennifer, Jerri-Lynn, Khea, Lucy, and Lulu as they navigated multiple contexts as post-secondary students on journeys of becoming teachers and researchers.[3] As we learned alongside one another we were particularly interested in understanding the shifts in each teacher's identities, their stories to live by, as they felt tensions with curricular, institutional, and structural plotlines that are often taken for granted aspects of post-secondary experiences for all students. Attending to these tensions was a way to understand how Aboriginal students are being educated to become teachers and researchers.

3.1. MOVING FORWARD IN RELATIONAL NARRATIVE INQUIRY

As shown in their earlier stories, while at differing times and places Janice and Mary searched for a research methodology that felt congruent with who they were each becoming and the inquiries they imagined, they both became drawn toward the relational aspects of narrative inquiry. As Clandinin and Connelly wrote: "Relationship is key to what it is that narrative inquirers do" (2000, p. 189). Key in negotiating relationships as narrative inquirers is our collective sharing of stories of experience. This relational storytelling shapes both shared vulnerability among storytellers as each person awakens to the complexity of lives being composed and recomposed and, too, a growing sense of working from, and with, stories as a way to shape personal, social, and institutional change (Clandinin & Connelly, 1998, 2000; Connelly & Clandinin, 2006). Clandinin and Connelly (1998) describe this kind of narrative change as taking shape in the following ways:

> For us, the promise of storytelling emerges when we move beyond regarding a story as a fixed entity and engage in conversations with our stories. The mere telling of a story leaves it as a fixed entity. It is in the inquiry, in our conversations with each other, with texts, with situations, and with other stories that we can come to retelling our stories and to reliving them. (p. 251)

Furthermore, Maenette Benham (2007) writes that

> the power of narrative is that, because it deeply explores the tensions of power by illuminating its collisions (e.g., differences of knowledge and practices), it reveals interesting questions that mobilize processes and resources that benefit native people and their communities. Indeed, the political impact of narrative cannot be dismissed. (pp. 513–514)

It is from within these shifting, uncertain, and often uneasy spaces shaped in this meeting and, at times, collisions of storied lives, in this meeting, for example, of individual's stories with the dominant social, cultural, linguistic, and institutional narratives which shape schools and universities that "the only way to seek justice ... [is] through the power of the stories" (Marmon Silko, 1996, p. 20). As described by Marie Battiste and James (Sa'ke'j) Youngblood Henderson (2000),

> Stories are enfolding lessons. Not only do they transmit validated experiences; they also renew, awaken, and honour spiritual forces. Hence, almost every ancient story does not explain; instead it focuses on processes of knowing. (p. 77)

This power of stories is important throughout the unfolding of a narrative inquiry, from being in the field and composing field texts, to composing interim and research texts (Clandinin & Connelly, 2000). This power is also important in the subsequent interactions between narrative research texts and their readers, particularly when, as Molly Andrews (2007) raises, the stories revealed "are distant from experiences ... we ourselves may have encountered not only in our own lives but in the accounts of others" (p. 489). Further, Andrews highlights the vitality of "narrative imagination" which becomes shaped in this meeting of differing stories: "If we wish to access the frameworks of meaning for others, we must be willing and able to imagine a world other than the one we know" (p. 489).

This potential for change grows as participants and narrative inquirers engage in the inquiry *in relation*, that is, as they compose lives as co-researchers, seeing as part of the inquiry, and therefore inquiring into, tensions that arise in the negotiation of all phases of the inquiry, including within the co-composition of field, interim, and research texts (Clandinin, Murphy, Huber, & Murray Orr, 2010; Sweetland, Huber, & Keats Whelan, 2004). As highlighted earlier because change is central in narrative inquiry and "not merely the telling of stories" (Clandinin & Connelly, 1998, p. 246), asking questions, such as: "How will we retell our stories with new insights? ... How will we relive them with changed practices in our lives?" (p. 250) is at the heart of the processes we engage in as co-researchers in relational narrative inquiries. It is from within these kinds of engagements with our stories that attention turns toward questions of our multiple relational responsibilities as narrative inquirers (Clandinin & Connelly, 2000), relational responsibilities that stretch indefinitely into the long-term unfolding of lives (Huber, Clandinin, & Huber, 2006).

As he inquires into ways stories inform our knowing of ourselves and our interactions with others, Thomas King (2003), too, writes of our need to stay wakeful to our long-term relational responsibilities as we engage with stories. For example, at the end of the story he tells of Charm, a character in his book, King writes:

> Take Charm's story, for instance. It's yours. Do with it what you will. Tell it to friends. Turn it into a television movie. Forget it. But don't say in the years to come that you would have lived your life differently if only you had heard this story.
> You've heard it now. (p. 29)

In our living of our narrative inquiry we stayed ever wakeful to our long-term relational responsibilities to and with one another, to and with the lives of past and future generations of Aboriginal teachers, and to and with past and future generations of Aboriginal children, youth, families, Elders, and communities. As described by Linda Tuhiwai Smith (1999), there is global need for the history of Indigenous and non-Indigenous peoples to be *re*written as a way of *re*righting how we are positioned in the past, how we are positioned in the present, and how we might be positioned in the future. Central in this process of retelling history as a way to shape a more equitable and just, a more hope-filled future for Aboriginal teachers, children, youth, families, Elders, and communities is that Indigenous people "tell our own stories, write our own versions, in our own ways, for our own purposes" (p. 28). Increasingly throughout our narrative inquiry, we grew in our understandings that without attending to long-term relational responsibilities it is unlikely that significant change will happen. It is for this reason that in the upcoming chapters we call ourselves and readers to stay wakeful to our long-term relational responsibilities, that is, we ask ourselves, and readers: Now that we/you know these stories, what strengths, what responsibilities do we/you now carry? How might we/you live our/your lives differently?

3.1.1. Thinking Narratively With Stories of Experience

As Mary and Janice participated at the earlier described research issues table and narrative inquiry course, learning to share and inquire into their and others' stories of experience, they were gradually learning to think narratively about experience (Clandinin & Connelly, 2000). For Clandinin and Connelly (2000), thinking narratively about experience entails staying attentive to the multidimensionality of experience, that is, to the interaction among the personal and social, between the past, present, and future, and the place or places where an experience unfolded. As we collectively inquired into our stories to live by, staying wakeful to these dimensions of experience, we were increasingly drawn back to Mary's work in relation with intergenerational narrative reverberations (Young, 2003, 2005b). As shown earlier by Mary, one harmful legacy of the lingering narrative of colonization in the unfolding lives of Aboriginal people in Canada is the intergenerational narrative reverberations continuing to shape successive generations. These intergenerational narrative reverberations include the loss of language, traditional cultural knowledge, and spiritual and relational practices, particularly family relationships. Holding this understanding of intergenerational narrative reverberations in the foreground of our narrative inquiry shaped a way to stay attentive to the dominant curricular, institutional, and structural narratives shaping the experiences of Jennifer, Jerri-Lynn, Khea, Lucy, Lulu, and Brenda Mary. In this way we began to trace the intergenerational narrative reverberations of colonization continuing to shape the curricular, the institutional, and the structural narratives with which Jerri-Lynn, Khea, Lucy, Lulu, Brenda Mary, and Jennifer came into conflict. However, as we continued to stay attentive to the intergenerational narrative reverberations of colonization made visible in the stories of experiences shared by Khea, Lucy, Lulu, Brenda Mary, Jennifer, and Jerri-Lynn, all the while consciously asking questions of our long-term relational responsibilities to and with one another, and to and with Aboriginal and non-Aboriginal children, youth, families, Elders, and communities, another aspect of intergenerational narrative reverberations gradually became visible. This aspect, similar to Hilde Lindemann Nelson's (1995) sense of the potential of counterstories to resist and undermine a dominant narrative supported us to understand more about intergenerational narrative reverberations. Lindemann Nelson wrote that:

> Counterstories take what has (for the moment, at least) been determined, undo it, and reconfigure it with new moral significance. All dominant stories already contain within them the possibilities for this kind of undoing; it is in the nature of a narrative never to close down completely the avenues for its own subversion. The construction, revision, and reinterpretation that are ongoing in dominant storytelling leave plenty of opportunities for counterstories to weave their way inside. (p. 34)

As we brought Lindemann Nelson's understanding of the possibilities of "undoing" dominant narratives alongside the intergenerational narrative reverberations and long-term relational responsibilities made visible in Lucy's, Lulu's, Brenda Mary's, Jennifer's, Jerri-Lynn's, and Khea's stories to live by, our attention turned toward the reverberations each story *could have* in the "subversion" of the dominant narrative of colonization. In this way, we saw that each experience carried within it the possibility for additional alternative reverberations, reverberations seeking to counter, to interrupt, the lingering narrative of colonization and to start new possible narrative reverberations in the lives of present and future generations of Aboriginal and non-Aboriginal teachers, children, youth, families, and communities.

3.2. NEGOTIATING RELATIONAL NARRATIVE INQUIRY WITHIN AND ACROSS MULTIPLE LIVES AND PLACES

In the summer of 2005, as we received institutional research ethics approval to begin our narrative inquiry, as well as ethical and cultural approval from the *Mi'kmaq* Ethics Watch,[4] Mary and Janice simultaneously met with Elders and with post-secondary students studying in undergraduate and graduate teacher education programs, inviting each person to consider collaborating in our inquiry. Lulu, Brenda Mary, Jennifer, Jerri-Lynn, Khea, and Lucy each accepted Janice's and Mary's invitations to participate in this narrative inquiry as co-researchers. In Mary's and Janice's invitations to Sister Dorothy and Florence they asked that they, too, journey alongside as co-researchers, providing cultural, ethical, and spiritual guidance as our inquiry unfolded. They also asked Jean Clandinin to journey alongside as a narrative inquiry elder, supporting us to keep thinking narratively as our inquiry unfolded. From the outset, Florence, Sister Dorothy, and Jean lived in indelible ways within our narrative inquiry. As others have noted (Ermine, Sinclair, & Jeffery, 2004; Menzies, 2004; Smith, 1999), the presence of Indigenous Elders in education and in research involving Aboriginal people is vital. In her Indigenous storywork alongside Elders, Jo-Ann Archibald (2008) writes of the guidance she sought and received from the Elders with whom she inquired:

> I recall the good warm feelings of being loved and respected by the Elders' Council that day. Going home.
>   They liked my work and said it was important to do; so many Elders have left us. We talked about the importance of stories for teaching and how they help us to live

right – to be good human beings. Such a relief not to be doing this important work alone, but to have guides. (p. 61)

Because we hoped our inquiry might also further develop narrative inquiry methodologies appropriate to, and respectful of, the knowledges and perspectives of Aboriginal people, all aspects of our inquiry have been strengthened through the sustained presence and full participation of Florence and Sister Dorothy. Archibald (2001) encourages Aboriginal people "to continue sharing our experiences, reflections and perspectives about cultural frameworks that facilitate a process of learning about and then appreciating Aboriginal knowledge and epistemology" (p. 2). It was in these ways that the presence of each Elder was significant.

At the beginning of each narrative inquiry circle, in both Nova Scotia and Manitoba, and at the beginning of each whole group narrative inquiry circle, Sister Dorothy and Florence began with prayers to the Creator, opening words or thoughts. These moments shaped a sense of quietness, a spiritual place to listen inwardly and outwardly as stories were shared, a place in which our stories mattered both as a way to understand the past and present, and as a way to imagine the future. Always, the emotion, the pain, the anger, the joy, the laughter, and the tensions that entered into the spaces shaped in the meeting of our storied lives, were valued; so, too, were our tears and our, at times, quietness. In these ways we grew, individually and collectively, in our understanding of the sacredness of story, in our understanding of our need, as described by David Bouchard and Joseph Martin (with illustrations by Kristy Cameron and music from Swampfox, 2009), to "be open to All Your Relations, so that through them you can walk your journey through life along the Good Red Road" (no page number). As we read this book well into our narrative inquiry, we were particularly drawn to Bouchard et al.'s retelling of White Calf Woman's seven sacred teachings, calling human beings to compose our lives with humility, honesty, respect, courage, wisdom, truth, and love. These are teachings that cannot be realized unless we "open ... [our] heart[s] and listen" (no page number), a process central as we seek to realize and understand ways of moving forward in good ways. As a way to both show and honour the vital presences of Florence and Sister Dorothy's ongoing guidance and significant participation in our narrative inquiry their stories, which were often shared in the midst of a narrative inquiry circle when we most needed to keep thinking with our stories to imagine ways forward, encircle the four upcoming chapters: *Reclaiming and Maintaining Our Aboriginal Ancestry*; *Reclaiming Our Ancestral Knowledge and Ways:*

Aboriginal Teachers Honouring Children, Youth, Families, Elders, and Communities as Relational Decision Makers; *Becoming "Real" Aboriginal Teachers: Counterstories as Shaping New Curriculum Making Possibilities*; and *Being Included In and Balancing the Complexities of Becoming An Aboriginal Teacher*.

Through all phases of our narrative inquiry Jean has also been alongside us as our narrative inquiry elder, supporting our inquiry in multiple ways. At the beginning of our inquiry, when Mary and Janice wrote the grant application which funded our inquiry, Jean was alongside, providing significant guidance in the ways we framed our application and inquiry. When, some months later, we learned that our grant application was successful, Jean talked with Janice and Mary around some of the tensions they were experiencing as the more relational ethics of narrative inquiry rubbed up against some of the less relational aspects of the university research ethics applications. As the grounding of university research ethics applications are often quite different, and sometimes, come into direct conflict with the ethical understandings of relational narrative inquiry (Clandinin & Connelly, 2000; Craig & Huber, 2007; Huber & Clandinin, 2002), these ongoing conversations with Jean were vital. In the summer of 2007, after 2 years of engaging in intensive narrative inquiry circles in both Manitoba and Nova Scotia, and by that time, one whole group research meeting, Jean met with Mary and Janice to support our beginning to think about the possibilities of co-authoring a book. In the midst of each of our busy lives, having Jean encourage this process and space in our inquiry was invaluable. While all along Jean has asked to not be named as an actual co-author of our book, she has, in numerous ways, lived deeply alongside in this co-composition, including participating in each of the whole group narrative inquiry circles.

3.3. CO-MAKING OUR RELATIONAL NARRATIVE INQUIRY ALONG THE WAY

We began meeting in our two narrative inquiry circles, Mary with Brenda Mary, Jennifer, Jerri-Lynn, and Florence in Winnipeg and Janice with Khea, Lucy, Lulu, and Sister Dorothy in Membertou, in the fall of 2005. Meeting approximately every 2 weeks for the following 2 years, and then less intensively into the third and fourth years of our collaboration, each group shaped narrative inquiry processes that felt respectful and safe. In many ways, we tried to shape narrative inquiry spaces similar to the research issues table we earlier described. For example, in between their twice monthly narrative inquiry circles Mary, Brenda Mary, Jennifer, Jerri-Lynn, and Florence wrote journals. These journal entries sometimes reflected on aspects raised in earlier narrative inquiry circles. At other times the journal entries were shaped by situations experienced in university classes, schools, family or community contexts and that seemed connected with and important to think about as part of our narrative inquiry. At subsequent meetings the journal entries were shared and inquired into within the circle. Mary also read and responded to each person's journal, responding in ways in which she storied her life experiences as a way to encourage Jennifer, Jerri-Lynn, Brenda Mary, and Florence to stay strong and to continue writing as a way to know who they each were and who they were each becoming.

Early in their twice monthly narrative inquiry circles Janice, Khea, Lucy, Lulu, and Sister Dorothy decided to audio record their conversations and to have transcripts made from the recordings. They also, at times, shared photographs and memory box artifacts during their conversations, items described by Clandinin and Connelly (1994) as "triggers to our memories, to recollecting the 'little fragments that have no beginning and no end' ... and around which we tell and retell stories. It is these artifacts collected in our lives that provide a rich source of memories" (p. 165). For example, as they began a narrative inquiry circle on December 1, 2007, Sister Dorothy shared with Khea, Lucy, Lulu, and Janice, the following poem:

> The
> Universe
> Yet incomplete
> On the sixth day GOD created her
> Woman
> And God said to her
> I shall give to you
> A heart full of compassion
> A spirit free to fly with the birds
> A vessel to carry life into the world
> Wisdom to know great truths
> Courage to rise out of oppression
> Strength to move mountains
> Gentleness to kiss the earth
> Passion to set the world on fire
> Vision to respect the world that bore you
> A playful nature to dance with the children
> Laughter to fill the valleys

Tears to wash the pain away
Hands for laboring and loving
Intuition to know the unknown
Desire to be that which you were created to be and God said to her
Woman
I have created you in my image and likeness and
You are
Good
(Poem shared by Sister Dorothy in a narrative inquiry circle on December 1, 2007)

After reading the poem aloud together, Sister Dorothy asked Khea, Lucy, Lulu, and Janice to each choose a phrase that spoke to them and to share their thoughts with one another. This artifact and their sharing in relation with it drew forward stories of their experiences as mothers, partners, teachers, daughters, sisters, and so on; stories of awakening to their strengths, the significance of their friendships with one another over time, and of ways they carry the work of our narrative inquiry into other aspects of their lives as it shapes how they live in those spaces.

As we lived in each narrative inquiry circle we also engaged in reading that felt connected with wonders, questions, and tensions emerging during our inquiry. These readings included full books, such as: *Pimatisiwin: Walking in a Good Way – A Narrative Inquiry into Language as Identity* (Young, 2005b), *Finding My Talk: How Fourteen Canadian Native Women Reclaimed Their Lives After Residential School* (Grant, 2004). We also read sections from books or documents such as *Guidelines for Health Research Involving Aboriginal Peoples* (Canadian Institutes of Health Research, 2005), *Learning About Walking in Beauty: Placing Aboriginal Perspectives in Canadian Classrooms* (Canadian Race Relations, 2003), and *The Truth About Stories: A Native Narrative* (King, 2003). Our reading also included an assortment of papers, such as those written earlier and presented by Sister Dorothy: *Mi'kmaq* Language A Human Right (2002), From Exclusive to Inclusive Education (2004), and Validity of Native Spirituality (2001) as well as a paper written by Mary, Is the Legacy of Residential Schools Relevant Today? (2005a) and a paper coauthored by Janice, Relational Responsibilities as Narrative Inquirers (Huber et al., 2006). We also read and discussed picture books, including *The Meaning of Respect* (Bouchard, 1994) and *The Dot* (Reynolds, 2003), and poetry, such as We Teach (Joe, 2000, p. 52).

Once per year we gathered as a large narrative inquiry circle, spending a few intense days together as we strengthened our relationships and talked about our narrative inquiry processes and emerging insights. These times were significant and special; they were marked by much laughter, many tears, and growing strength shaped through story and relationships, the wisdom and prayers of Sister Dorothy and Florence, and the ongoing response and encouragement of Jean. Our whole group narrative inquiry circles also supported us in becoming more wakeful to the multiple resonant threads emerging across the storied lives of Jennifer, Jerri-Lynn, Khea, Lucy, Lulu, and Brenda Mary. As mentioned earlier, Jean met with Mary and Janice in summer 2007 to encourage our development of a book based on the stories resonating across our narrative inquiry circles. In the fall of 2007, at our second whole group narrative inquiry circle, we discussed and further developed the ideas for each chapter. During the remainder of 2007 and most of 2008, Mary and Janice worked with all of the field texts from our two narrative inquiry circles, the journal entries, and audio-recorded conversations, to pull forward possible stories with which to think narratively. As described by Clandinin and Connelly (2000) narratively coding field texts is a complex process.

> For example, names of the characters that appear in field texts, places where actions and events occurred, story lines that interweave and interconnect, gaps and silences that become apparent, tensions that emerge, and continuities and discontinuities that appear are all possible codes. As narrative researchers engage in this work, they begin to hold different field texts in relation to other field texts. (p. 131)

Throughout 2008 and 2009, as we continued to meet, although less frequently, in each small narrative inquiry circle we revisited each story. In hindsight we now see that in this revisiting of our earlier told stories we were living in the midst of gradually shifting our stories to live by toward retellings with the potential to shape new possible intergenerational narrative reverberations.

It was during this process of continuing to think with our collective stories, and in particular, with Jerri-Lynn's, Khea's, Lucy's, Lulu's, Brenda Mary's, and Jennifer's stories, that we often revisited the common use of pseudonyms in the sharing or publishing of research texts. As we started our narrative inquiry, within and across both narrative inquiry circles, there was a sense of needing pseudonyms. Yet, as time, relationships, and our narrative inquiry processes unfolded these pseudonyms, originally included on written journal entries and transcripts of audio-recorded conversations, slowly shifted. By the time we began sharing aspects of our narrative inquiry at conferences (Young et al., 2008) and co-authoring writing for publication (Young et al., 2010), our collective sense of needing to maintain confidentiality through the use of pseudonyms had shifted. In this writing we have consciously chosen to not cover over or hide anyone's life with pseudonyms. Each in their own ways and words, Brenda Mary, Jennifer, Jerri-Lynn, Khea, Lucy, and Lulu decided and described that sharing their stories with a broader audience was a way they are working to shape change for future generations of Aboriginal and non-Aboriginal teachers, children, youth, families, and communities. Becoming visible in both the living, and in this book which is one telling, of our narrative inquiry was a way for each teacher to show the responsibilities they feel for living by stories that will make a positive difference for those who come next. Each of Jennifer's, Jerri-Lynn's, Khea's, Lucy's, Lulu's, and Brenda Mary's individual decisions were shaped by a sense of needing to live by stories much bigger than themselves, stories that look toward the lives of future generations, stories that seek healing through storying and restorying personal, institutional, familial, and communal experiences.

At this same time we engaged in many conversations about the multiple languages in which our experiences were storied, both orally and in written formats. After months of thinking about ways of showing this aspect of our narrative inquiry we came to a shared sense of not hiding or silencing our multiple languages. Readers will experience these multiple languages throughout our book.

Our collective decision to represent our storied lives in the narrative form of word images, which were composed from the journal entries, transcripts, or audio recordings of our narrative inquiry circles, and which resemble found poetry (Butler-Kisber, 2002), was gradually shaped through our desires for our experiences to be deeply heard, to be experienced, by readers. Archibald (2008) gives a sense of what we were hoping for when she writes that

> Patience and trust are essential for preparing to listen to stories. Listening involves more than just using the auditory sense. We must visualize the characters and their actions. We must let our emotions surface. As Elders say, it is important to listen with "three ears: two on the sides of our head and the one that is in our heart." (2008, p. 8)

Word images are interim research texts (Clandinin & Connelly, 2000; Clandinin et al., 2006; Huber et al., 2011) which carry potential for showing the emotions storytellers experience as they live through experiences and, then, which they re-experience as these earlier lived experiences are storied and restoried.[5] In her description of the connections between poetry and the emotional aspects of experience Audre Lorde (1984) gives a sense of this, that is,

> Poetry is not a luxury but a vital necessity of our existence. It forms the quality of the light within which we predicate our hopes and dreams toward survival and change. ...

The farthest horizons of our hopes and fears are cobbled by our poems, carved from the rock experiences of our daily lives. (p. 37)

Our gradual decision to work with word images as a way to represent our stories began, then, as one way to show the complex, intergenerational, and at times, almost inarticulatable aspects of our storied lives. However, as we worked with word images over time we came to realize the potential cultural significance of the rhythmic nature of word images. When read aloud word images often shape a kind of beat similar to what we experience in our hearts when we hear the drum. In the upcoming chapters we ask readers to please consider speaking out loud the word images composed from our storied and restoried lives. In doing so, we hope that as readers see, hear, and feel our storied lives that our hopes and dreams for new possible intergenerational narrative reverberations will stay with you.

NOTES

1. This SSHRC grant was co-held by D. Jean Clandinin and F. Michael Connelly. I was involved as a post doctoral research assistant and co-researcher. Further details about this relational narrative inquiry are published in Clandinin et al. (2006), Huber and Clandinin (2005), Huber et al. (2003), and Huber et al. (2003).

2. We (J. Huber, D. J. Clandinin, M. Huber, K. Keats Whelan, D. Labbé, M. S. Murphy, & P. Steeves) received funding for this inquiry, *Reshaping Classroom and School Contexts: Learning From Stories of Aboriginal Children and Families*, from the Dr. Stirling McDowell Research Foundation, Saskatchewan Teachers' Federation.

3. Our narrative inquiry, *Negotiating Diverse Identities: Becoming Aboriginal Teachers and Researchers*, was supported by a grant to Mary Young and Janice Huber from the Social Sciences and Humanities Research Council of Canada (SSHRC).

4. The *Mi'kmaq* Ethics Watch includes the following description on their website: "A Mi'kmaq Ethics Committee has been appointed by the Sante Mawio'mi (Grand Council) to establish a set of principles and protocols that will protect the integrity and cultural knowledge of the Mi'kmaq people. These principles and protocols are intended to guide research and studies in a manner that will guarantee that the right of ownership rests with the various Mi'kmaq communities. These principles and protocols will guarantee only the highest standards of research. Interpretation and conclusions drawn from the research will be subject to approval to ensure accuracy and cultural sensitivity." (http://mrc.uccb.ns.ca/prinpro.html)

5. For further reading on word images please see Clandinin et al. (2006), Huber and Clandinin (2005), and Huber (2008).

CHAPTER 4

RECLAIMING AND MAINTAINING OUR ABORIGINAL ANCESTRY

The other day
On our drive to visit family on the reserve
I told my husband I haven't seen an eagle this year
Low and behold there was a bald eagle
My husband pulls over to the side of the road and we watch it as it circles around
    or above us
The eagle landed not far from my sister's, and sits perched on a tree facing north
I reach for the tobacco that I carry in my purse and we offer it
We both say a prayer of thanks as we are feeling very blessed
An eagle is a sacred bird to the *Anishinabe* people and when one is sighted a
    tobacco offering is made
I know about these special gifts our ancestors used to be able to do
They were able to [use their gifts] because they were strong spirited people
And
We are becoming [strong spirited people] too
(Word image composed from Florence's journal entries written on November 13,
2005 & October 31, 2007)

If an individual can't trust to say what it is that needs to be said
Things will never change
And we have to
I think
Have the confidence and fortitude and the risk
There's always a risk to say what needs to be said
Unless we
As individuals
Take that risk
The things that need to be changed
Will never change
(Word image composed from Sister Dorothy's experiences storied in a narrative inquiry
circle on February 24, 2008)

Our *Anishinabe* and *Mi'kmaq* Elders, Florence and Sister Dorothy, remind us that we have gifts. These gifts are our stories and it is through stories that we can connect with our ancestors. This intergenerational connection across time and place shapes strong spirited Aboriginal people. One aspect of the narrative of colonization imposed on Aboriginal people was breaking their spirits by taking away language, culture, relationships, values, and beliefs. While it often still feels risky, in many places and spaces, to live in ways that honour our Aboriginal ancestry by never giving up our stories has ensured that the connections from our ancestors to us and from us to future generations will not be lost. Our living of this narrative process, the storying and restorying of who we were, who we are, and who we can be as strong spirited Aboriginal people continues to be central in shaping a future of dignity and strength for all Aboriginal people (Archibald, 2008; Basso, 1996; Battiste & Henderson, 2000; Morris, 2002; Silko, 1996; Trinh, 1989).

And, so, we begin in storied lives ...

Jennifer

When I was as young as 6-years-old
I recognized I was "Indian"
Even though my concept of an Aboriginal person
Was someone who lived in a tipi and wore skins as clothes
I felt special
I was proud to be "Indian"
But I had no idea
What I was proud of

My attitude
And feelings
About being "Indian"
Have changed over time
And I came to a point
Where I resisted any further cultural understandings
Teachings
Or ventures

I am filled with feelings
Of doubt
Resentment
Jealousy
And defeat
When I think of Aboriginal people

Some days
I wish my skin
Did not label me
This way

Interesting
To look back on writing from our inquiry from a year ago
And to find
I am almost
In the same place
As I was then

I always come back to this place
To this state of mind
To this way of thinking
It's comfortable

I began to keep my thoughts
To myself
To not voice them

Aboriginal rights and the plight of Aboriginal people in Canada is such a huge
Messy
Hot
Topic
It is easier
To say
Nothing

I haven't had
A safe place
To battle out my opinions
So
I stopped thinking about them
Other Aboriginal people also haven't had
A safe place

I've come
Close
To being dissatisfied with my place
It is so easy to not think
And therefore do nothing

I'm now
Discovering
It is no longer acceptable
To stay in this place
Of comfort
This place of not expressing
Myself

I realize
We only learn

And grow
As people
By first
Not knowing
And second
By taking a risk
To experience
Something new

For me
To not think about Aboriginal issues in relation to Canadian society
And myself
As an Aboriginal person
And teacher
Would be stunting
My growth
Personally
And professionally
A failure to reflect would also impact my students
And could cause me to make the same mistakes my teachers did when I was
        growing up
This is not the story I want to live by
(Word image composed from Jennifer's journal entries written on November 8, 2005 &
October 28, 2006)

As a young child, Jennifer came to name herself as "Indian," an understanding of herself she linked with "living in a tipi and ... [wearing] skins as
clothes." Understanding herself in this way, Jennifer "felt special" and
"proud to be 'Indian'" even though she was not sure why. As she grew older,
Jennifer began to wish her "skin did not label" her as a person of Aboriginal
ancestry. In time, she became "filled with feelings of doubt, resentment,
jealousy, and defeat when ... [she thought] of Aboriginal people"; she
eventually began to live a story in which she resisted "any further cultural
understandings, teachings, or ventures." Jennifer stories herself as becoming
uncomfortable identifying with the dominant narrative about Aboriginal
peoples in Canada as she tried to figure out where she fit in her predominately
non-Aboriginal community.

Part way through her journaling process in our relational narrative
inquiry Jennifer revisited her first journal entry, adding to it how she now
understands ways the dominant narrative of colonizing Aboriginal people
continues to reverberate in her life. Across her two journal entries Jennifer
shows that her early feelings of being special and of being proud of her
ancestry gradually shifted to living by stories of silence. As she was growing
up, Jennifer learned it was "so easy to not think and therefore do nothing"

about "Aboriginal rights and the plight of Aboriginal people in Canada." Her growing silence was, in part, shaped because she felt as though she did not have a safe place to "battle out ... [her] opinions." In the absence of a safe place, Jennifer gradually chose to live by stories of comfort, stories that shaped her to not voice her opinions or to express herself. Without a safe place and growing up as she did in a time when the lives of Aboriginal people in Canada were a "huge, messy, hot topic," an era that continues to reverberate in her life as a teacher, Jennifer felt that her easiest choice was to live by stories in which she "stopped thinking." This intersection between the struggle of dominant social, cultural, and institutional narratives to come to terms with the history of the colonization of Aboriginal people in Canada alongside Jennifer's emerging stories to live by, shows how she learned to deny her thoughts and feelings. In time, it became "easier to say nothing."

Further to understanding the impact which the dominant narrative of colonization has shaped in her life, Jennifer recognizes the need to be an active participant in creating new stories. Jennifer shows that her emerging stories to live by are ones that help to change the dominant narrative and, in this way, to create new possibilities for all children in school. Jennifer also shows that the process of journaling and having a "safe place" to reflect upon her experiences supported her to realize the importance of her stories of experience. She describes this space and relationships as helping her to find courage to begin examining her thoughts and feelings, forming opinions and voicing them instead of remaining silent.

Lucy

In one of my classes the professor said to me:
"In order for you to succeed in life
You have to learn English"
I told him,
"Yes I know that might be true today
But I also know that statistics prove that having more than one language is better in a
    child's development"
I think the professor made this comment
Because another student gave a presentation about how necessary it is
For children
To learn French in schools
Everyone was talking about the presentation
I said,
"I can relate to that story because of the residential schools and how the language of
    my people
Was lost

Now
I don't have my language
And I, like a lot of *Mi'kmaq* people,
Am fighting
To get my language back"

The professor commented that in order for me to get anywhere
In life
I needed to learn English

The whole class went silent
For a long time
Then
The professor started to talk about something else
I felt like the professor
Was trying to downgrade
My opinion

I think it was important that I said what I did
That I did not hide
My disagreement with the professor
Even when it got silent
I did not feel uncomfortable
Because I strongly feel
That the loss of the *Mi'kmaq* language
Is as important
As the loss of the French language
Educators need to think about
Both

I really feel this professor
Was into himself
That he was only interested
In students
Who were interested
In him
It worries me that I will probably need to take another course from him
Before finishing the program
That will be hard
(Word image composed from Lucy's experiences storied in narrative inquiry circles on
September 8, 2007 & December 1, 2008)

Lucy, as an adult, mother, and teacher of *Maliseet* and *Mi'kmaq* ancestry, is "fighting to get ... [her] language back." This is not easy. However, when in a graduate course, she drew upon the complexity in her life shaped by the intergenerational loss of language as a result of the residential schools she felt "the professor was trying to downgrade ... [her] opinion." As she lived through these moments in the class Lucy felt the sense that the loss of the French language was somehow more significant, more urgent, than the loss of the *Mi'kmaq* language. In this way, English, again, still, was positioned as the only language she required in order "to succeed in life." As this living out of the dominant narrative of colonization of Aboriginal people shaped the classroom space of her graduate course, Lucy described the silence that pervaded the room. No one spoke. Then, the professor, without any response to Lucy's expression of ways in which the colonization of her ancestors was reverberating in her life, in her stories to live by, "started to talk about something else."

Jerri-Lynn

My group and I finished our presentation
On language loss
And presented it the day before yesterday
I think we did pretty good
I'm proud of how well
We worked together
Now
That we're actually getting into the meat of this program
I am so excited to be here
Learning my mother's language
To be able to read
And write it
I totally embrace my Aboriginal heritage
I grew up in the city
And
I was not taught about traditional ways
Of life
I never knew much about Aboriginal culture
I am willing to learn
And
Respect it
(Word image composed from Jerri-Lynn's journal entries written on November 3 & 9, 2005)

In her two earlier journal entries Jerri-Lynn traces her upbringing and associates the current stories she lives by as shaped because she grew up in the city and was not "taught about traditional ways of life" or "never knew much about Aboriginal culture." Jerri-Lynn's experiences are not surprising given that educational policies concerning Aboriginal people were strongly influenced by the dominant narrative of colonizing Aboriginal people. In the precursor to residential schools, in the industrial schools set up to educate Aboriginal children, it is well documented that central in the process of changing their identities, the stories to live by of Aboriginal children, they were taken and "insulated" from their families and communities. The intentions within this process were to have the children forget who they were and where they came from; it was intended that the children would simply take on the stories their teachers lived by in the industrial or residential schools (Young, 2005a).

Lulu

We've got to fight for our language
And for who we are as *Mi'kmaq* people

I remember going to public high school
I have bad memories of going there
I never want to go back there
When we first went there
We kept to ourselves
We all spoke *Mi'kmaq*
One day I decided to go to the cafeteria to eat
I saw a table where no one else was sitting
I sat there
Someone tapped me on the shoulder
And said,
"Excuse me you're in my chair"
I looked up at her
She had a few friends along
I said
"But you weren't sitting here"
I turned back around
She tapped me again
And said,
"You're in my chair. You better leave now"
I thought to myself
"I'm not moving"
She hit me
I hit her back
I was suspended for three days
My grandfather asked what happened
He wondered if she hit me first
I said she had
He said
"Okay, it's alright then
Never punch first but if they throw the first punch then you punch back"

The second time I was suspended
Was because of a teacher
I had just received my status card

I was very proud of it
I was 16
In Grade 11
And my status card was in my school bag
The history teacher said
"Oh, you'll see Indians down at wherever shopping and flashing these status cards
    as if they are credit cards"
I took out my status card
I stood up
And said
"Does it look like this?"
Then I sat back down and threw a book at him
I was suspended for three days

We got to the school by bus
By the time the bus arrived at the high school
It was covered in eggs
The bus driver would never let us off
If students were standing around when we pulled up
Because sometimes
Students threw rocks and eggs
At us

After all the racism
Fighting
And suspensions
I experienced in the public high school
I loved the university where I did my first degree
I felt safe there
It felt like a second home

During my B. Ed. (after-degree)
The professors wanted me to go to this same public high school
For practicum
I said
"No!"

Now
In a graduate course
We were all sitting in a circle
Each student was asked to talk about something in their paper
The professor had all of these quotes that she really liked from our papers
She had this quote about how kindergarten children are like flowers or like soft
    petals
And you can either blow or care for the petals
I said I wanted to talk about that quote because I thought it was important

Two other *Mi'kmaq* students
Were also sitting in the circle
I immediately started to speak in *Mi'kmaq*
Saying I wanted to talk about my experiences in kindergarten
And my hands were going and I started to tell my stories
But one of the other *Mi'kmaq* students
Interrupted me
And said,
"Lulu, speak in English"
I did not even look at her
I kept talking
In *Mi'kmaq*
Telling my stories of kindergarten
When I finished some of the other students said it was very powerful
They said they had to look at my body
To try to understand
What I was saying
They said they could feel
When I was talking about
Something sad
And when
I was talking about
Something happy

In English then
I told everyone in the circle
My story was that
When I started school
My teacher was an English speaker
And I did not understand English
I said
My reason for telling my story
In *Mi'kmaq*
Was so they could
Maybe
Understand some of what my experience in school was like
I said
"You know
As educators
We have to consider that not all of us speak the same language
Or learn in the same ways"
(Word image composed from Lulu's experiences storied in narrative inquiry circles,
January 28, 2006 & September 8, 2007)

Early in our relational narrative inquiry, Lulu storied her memories of
ways in which the intergenerational narrative reverberation of colonization
shaped her experiences in a public high school where she felt unaccepted,

alienated, and mistreated because of racism toward *Mi'kmaq* people. These experiences were shaped not only as she interacted with peers but, as well, with a teacher and with the administrator who suspended her from school. Over a full year later, and many years after she attended the public high school, Lulu storied her recent participation in one of the final courses in her master's program, telling of how, as she consciously chose to speak in *Mi'kmaq*, another student, also of *Mi'kmaq* ancestry, interrupted and urged her to "speak in English."

Brenda Mary

I ask myself if this is where
I am meant to be
Or am I running into
A brick wall?
I feel like
Every day
Is a challenge for me
I do not even know
How to write
Right
The right way I mean
I want to learn all these skills
So I can reach my goal
To teach the language
But I have to learn it
First
I find it to be such a task to come up with answers to questions
I don't even understand
In language planning
We need to read a chapter
And answer 3 of 6 questions
No one in the class
Finished that assignment
That tells me
I need to understand the questions
By rewording them
Then
See if I understand them
Then
Answer them
Each question needs to have
At least one page
It is overwhelming
For me

When I shared in our meeting about the language
That is my passion
To learn the language
And to give it back
By teaching
It is my dream
My goal
And what I am shooting for
No one can take that from me
I need to heal
From the loss
Of language
And
The way I am doing that
Is by learning the language

We have it within our power
Now
To shape our own destiny
We can take
This education
And use it
In a good way
To walk the good road
Like your book
Mary
I remember teachers who were a couple
They had a reel-to-reel tape recorder
A big thing in those days
They recorded my father's father playing fiddle
My grandfather used to get us to dance jig
He would play the fiddle
We danced jig
To red river jig
And
Other tunes

I go on
Today
With these kinds of memories
Ancestral energy
And passions
Revitalizing
Renewing
The language of the people
Anishinaabe
(Word image composed from Brenda Mary's journal entries written on October 20, 2006 &
October 13, 2007)

As Brenda Mary shows in her earlier journal entries, the intergenerational narrative reverberation of the colonization of Aboriginal people shaped her life as a child. Even now, this intergenerational narrative reverberation of colonization continues to shape Brenda Mary's life and her stories to live by as a grandmother through the loss in her family and community of the *Anishinaabe* language. This intergenerational narrative reverberation continues as Brenda Mary, now on a journey of becoming a teacher with passions to heal herself and her community by wanting to return to the community to teach the language to present and future generations of children, struggles in an institution where there seems to be little recognition of the complex process in which she needs to engage as she tries to "answer 3 of 6 questions." As she storied this experience Brenda Mary realized she was overwhelmed and, like other students in the course, was not able to finish the assignment because in order "to understand the questions" she needed, first, to "reword them" into English, after which, she needed to write a one-page response. As she navigated this institutional narrative shaping this post-secondary place Brenda Mary did not feel as though she had a space to share her stories of this experience. Instead, she carried her stories within herself. In doing so, Brenda Mary slowly began to feel lost in the contradictions of the post-secondary education she was experiencing.

Khea

Mi'kmaq
Was my first language
But I stopped speaking it all of the time
When I was 3 or 4
I liked the way I sounded when I spoke English
My mom used to tell me
If I spoke *Mi'kmaq*
I was going to have a much more difficult time
In the future
She wanted me
To have minimal difficulties
In school
Her reason was that I would succeed better if I was equipped with the English language
I know my mom told me this
Because she loved me
She wanted me
To be happy
When I grew up
But
Today

My parents
Feel sorry
They let me speak English
But
That was their generation
When I was growing up
Because of the residential schools
Many parents told their children
Not to speak *Mi'kmaq*

As an adult
I have relearned
The *Mi'kmaq* language

I started to relearn the *Mi'kmaq* language
When I went to university
I met this guy and he said to me
"Alright, I want to hear your language. Count to ten"
So I counted to ten
Then he said
"Now count to a hundred"
But I couldn't
And I had to say so
He said
"You should be ashamed
Of yourself
You
Are a *Mi'kmaq* person
And you can't even count to a hundred"
That hit home for me
I was embarrassed
And
I was ashamed
I had become so English

Now
As a parent
I am ensuring that both my daughters
Speak *Mi'kmaq*
In our community there is a *Mi'kmaq* immersion program
From Kindergarten to the end of Grade 3
I am thrilled my daughters
Can learn their language in a program like this
My oldest daughter
She's in her graduating year
This year
From the Grade 3 *Mi'kmaq* immersion program
She's in the second group of children

To be in the immersion program
She can read
So well
She just looks at something
And she knows if she's written it
Right
Or wrong
(Word image composed from Khea's experiences storied in a narrative inquiry circle, January 28, 2006)

The lingering pain of the intergenerational narrative reverberation of the colonization of Khea's ancestors is strongly voiced in her earlier told story. It is an intergenerational narrative reverberation that shaped Khea's young life as she gradually learned to not speak *Mi'kmaq* and to like "the way ... [she] sounded when ... [she] spoke English." As she remembered how her early stories to live by were shaped and reshaped Khea reflected on her mother's love for her. Khea described how her mother wanted her "to have minimal difficulties in school." At the time when Khea began school the language of instruction was English and her mom believed that Khea would "succeed better" if she "was equipped with the English language." Today, however, both Khea and her parents "feel sorry they let ... [Khea] speak in English." As Khea shows, her parents' lives and their decision to encourage her to speak English "was their generation." When she was growing up, "because of the residential schools" and the intentional focus of these institutions on taking away Aboriginal languages and replacing them with English "many parents told their children not to speak in *Mi'kmaq*."

In her story as well Khea makes visible ways in which the intergenerational narrative reverberation of the colonization of Aboriginal people has shaped the lives of non-Aboriginal people in Canada. As she attended university and met someone who asked her to "count to 10" and then "to a hundred," Khea felt she needed to say she could not count to a hundred. This person's response, "You should be ashamed of yourself, you are a *Mi'kmaq* person and you can't even count to a hundred," shows how the narrative of the colonization of Aboriginal people was reverberating in the stories he lived by. In this person's stories it seemed as though he held no knowledge of ways in which the colonization of Aboriginal people in Canada is continuing to reverberate in his and Khea's generation. Instead, he seemed to understand Khea's loss of her language as a deficiency within herself, her family, and her community. He also seems unaware that he, too, through the intergenerational narrative reverberations in his family, may have lost the language and ways of knowing in which his ancestors knew and communicated their stories, their lives.

4.1. TAKING RESPONSIBILITY: RECLAIMING ABORIGINAL ANCESTRY AND LANGUAGE THROUGH THE COMPOSITION OF COUNTER STORIES TO LIVE BY

As Jennifer, Lucy, Jerri-Lynn, Lulu, Brenda Mary, and Khea storied and restoried their lives in the ways earlier noted, we were in the midst of, as earlier noted, gradually growing in our wakefulness of attending to new possible intergenerational narrative reverberations made visible in their storied lives, in their stories to live by. As they storied their lives Jennifer, Lucy, Jerri-Lynn, Lulu, Brenda Mary, and Khea not only taught us of ways in which the intergenerational narrative reverberation of colonizing Aboriginal people continues to reverberate in their lives, in their stories to live by, but they also showed us the new possible intergenerational narrative reverberations they are composing. These new possible intergenerational narrative reverberations are poised to counter and to restory the colonization and oppression of Aboriginal people. In this way, by tracing the counter stories to live by they are composing so as to shape new possible intergenerational narrative reverberations we see that their counterstories to live by carry much potential for shaping a future in which the spirits of Aboriginal teachers, children, youth, families, and communities in Canada are strong.

In the midst of our narrative inquiry Jennifer experienced a safe place where she could "battle out ... [her] opinions." Through our relational narrative inquiry process Jennifer storied her growing wakefulness to the tensions shaped within herself when she does not speak or express herself. As she attended over time to her tensions with this aspect of her life, Jennifer restoried her stories to live by as she determined that it was no longer acceptable to stay in a place of comfort, in a place of not expressing herself. To not think about Aboriginal issues in relation to Canadian society and herself as an Aboriginal person and teacher would be, to Jennifer, a process of stunting her growth personally and professionally, a process of living by stories of silence. In this restorying of her stories to live by Jennifer is moving toward a future shaped by a sense of needing to speak. Storying and restorying these hard-to-tell experiences in her life became a way for Jennifer to live responsibly with herself and the knowledge she carries because of her ancestors across multiple generations alongside her unfolding life experiences.

Neither the professor nor students in the graduate course said anything as Lucy tried to show the significance in her life and in the lives of future generations of children, of learning *Mi'kmaq*. Even though her response to the professor that "having more than one language is better in a child's development" was met with silence, months later, as she storied this experience, and then even more months later as she revisited and relived the experience, Lucy remained strong in her belief that what she had said was important. As she looked ahead to the completion of her master's degree, Lucy worried that she would need to take another course from this professor. She knew this would "be hard" but was prepared for further "uncomfortable" conversations or moments that might unfold in relation with him. What gave Lucy strength as she looked ahead was her strong belief "that the loss of the *Mi'kmaq* language is as important as the loss of the French language." Lucy was, as well, adamant that educators need to be attentive to language loss among all children and within many families and communities. In each of these ways Lucy was in the midst of composing counter stories to live by holding potential for shaping new possible intergenerational narrative reverberations poised to interrupt the ongoing colonization of Aboriginal people.

Jerri-Lynn's excitement to learn "her mother's language, to be able to read, and write it" spilled out onto the pages of her November 3rd and 5th, 2005, journal entries. Jerri-Lynn both wrote and talked about her willingness to learn and her respect for her mother's language and culture. In one of her post-secondary classes, a place predominately shaped by First Nations and Metis students, Jerri-Lynn found a space to create and share a group presentation on "language loss," an intergenerational narrative reverberation that has shaped her life through her mother's life. Jerri-Lynn expressed her joy in this opportunity to learn about an aspect of history so significant in her life and in her Aboriginal heritage. She wrote: "I totally embrace my Aboriginal heritage." As she, in this post-secondary place, awakened to a counterstory she could live by in response to the intergenerational narrative reverberation of the colonization of her ancestors, herself, and her children, Jerri-Lynn immersed herself in learning about her *Cree* culture and language. In this space she felt an increased sense of freedom from the policies imposed on her mother, and subsequently, onto Jerri-Lynn, policies meant to insulate her from her ancestors and their ways of knowing and being. With all of her being, Jerri-Lynn moved forward by clinging to anything she was able to learn about her people, knowledge that simultaneously supports her to restory her childhood experiences of not knowing who she was.

Lulu's unfolding stories, which chronicle her early schooling experiences in Kindergarten, high school, a first degree, a B.Ed. after-degree, and in a master's degree in education, show her growing strength to live by counter-stories to the intergenerational narrative reverberations of colonization. As she attended a public high school, even though she was suspended because she stood up for herself, at home she gained strength from her grandfather who encouraged her to not allow herself to be mistreated and silenced. In a subsequent classroom situation where she experienced the racism of a teacher, again Lulu stood her ground. The bus driver was one person in the high school whom Lulu trusted. He was a person she described as not letting the *Mi'kmaq* students off the bus "if [non-*Mi'kmaq*] students were standing around when we pulled up because sometimes ... [they] threw rocks and eggs at us."

After living through these experiences in the midst of the intergenerational narrative reverberations of racism shaping the high school she attended, Lulu described the university where she undertook her first degree as "a second home"; it was a place where she "felt safe." In the second university where Lulu studied to become a teacher she again composed a counter story to live by when she refused to accept a field placement in the public high school she had attended much earlier. In this post-secondary place, Lulu's refusal was both accepted and respected. And again, this time as a graduate student in a post-secondary place, Lulu's spirit, her stories to live by, were honoured as she found a space to share a hard story of her experiences as a young girl entering into a public school Kindergarten classroom, a story she shared in *Mi'kmaq*. The non-*Mi'kmaq* students in the course expressed important learning through Lulu's sharing in her language. Even though they did not know the meanings of the words she spoke in *Mi'kmaq*, they expressed to Lulu the deep feelings they experienced as she storied her early life experiences. Lulu was hopeful that the non-*Mi'kmaq* members of the course would carry these feelings forward into their teaching lives alongside young people who may not all "speak the same language or learn in the same ways."

As an *Anishinabe* post-secondary student on a journey of becoming a teacher, Brenda Mary's "passion [is] to learn the language and to give it back by teaching." This "is ... [her] dream," this is her "goal." The strength of her determination to begin a new possible intergenerational narrative reverberation that counters the intergenerational narrative reverberation of the colonization of Aboriginal people was evident as she wrote: "what I am shooting for, no one can take that from me. I need to heal from the loss of language and the way I am doing that is by learning it." Drawing on the "ancestral energy and passions" she reconnected with as she remembered earlier experiences with her grandfather and father and "danc[ing] jig,"

Brenda Mary took back the power stolen from her ancestors through colonization to "shape ... [both her] own destiny" and also, the destinies of the children and youth in her community. For Brenda Mary "revitalizing, renewing the language of the people, *Anishinaabe*" was powerfully reshaping her stories to live by. As she composed these new stories to live by in her present life, Brenda Mary was simultaneously looking toward to a future where the children and youth in her community would also be able to live by this new possible intergenerational narrative reverberation as they attended the school in their community, a place where they would be supported to learn, to speak, to think, to know in and through their *Anishinabe* language.

In the interaction Khea described with the person at the university who left her feeling "embarrassed" and "ashamed" for becoming "so English," her stories to live by began to shift. As Khea's stories to live by shifted she became committed to the new possible intergenerational narrative reverberation shaping herself, her parents, community, and school, a new possible intergenerational narrative reverberation of learning and speaking *Mi'kmaq*. While some years passed between this experience with a post-secondary colleague and Khea becoming a parent, her deep recognition of the importance of ensuring that her two daughters speak *Mi'kmaq* was not washed away. Today, in part, because "there is a *Mi'kmaq* Immersion program from Kindergarten to the end of Grade 3" in the community, Khea's daughters who are in school are fluent *Mi'kmaq* speakers. But their fluency in *Mi'kmaq* is also shaped because in her generation, different from her parents' generation, Khea has been gradually nurtured to be proud of who she is as a *Mi'kmaq* person who speaks her language. Khea's daughters are flourishing as they are nurtured to compose their identities, their stories to live by in a family place, a community place, and a school place supportive of *Mi'kmaq* language and culture.

If an individual can't trust to say what it is that needs to be said
Things will never change
And we have to
I think
Have the confidence and fortitude and the risk
There's always a risk to say what needs to be said
Unless we
As individuals
Take that risk
The things that need to be changed
Will never change

(Word image composed from Sister Dorothy's experiences storied in a narrative inquiry
circle on February 24, 2008)

The other day
On our drive to visit family on the reserve
I told my husband I haven't seen an eagle this year
Low and behold there was a bald eagle
My husband pulls over to the side of the road and we watch it as it circles around
    or above us
The eagle landed not far from my sister's, and sits perched on a tree facing north
I reach for the tobacco that I carry in my purse and we offer it
We both say a prayer of thanks as we are feeling very blessed
An eagle is a sacred bird to the *Anishinabe* people and when one is sighted a
    tobacco offering is made
I know about these special gifts our ancestors used to be able to do
They were able to [use their gifts] because they were strong spirited people
And
We are becoming [strong spirited people] too
(Word image composed from Florence's journal entries written on November 13,
2005 & October 31, 2007)

*Who can deny that the intergenerational narrative reverberations of
colonization have not shaped Brenda Mary's, Jennifer's, Jerri-Lynn's, Khea's,
Lucy's, and Lulu's lives, past and present? In storying their lives they show this
intergenerational shaping but, in their storying and restorying they also show
additional aspects of their lives. In their living, today, Jennifer, Lucy, Jerri-
Lynn, Lulu, Brenda Mary, and Khea are composing stories to live by that seek
to counter, to interrupt the harm done to them and to their ancestors.
Jennifer's, Lucy's, Jerri-Lynn's, Lulu's, Brenda Mary's, and Khea's counter
stories to live by are filled with possibilities for shaping new possible
intergenerational narrative reverberations. Will you walk alongside Jennifer,
Lucy, Jerri-Lynn, Lulu, Brenda Mary, and Khea? Will you become part of the
cultural, familial, linguistic, institutional, and social restorying to which they
are reaching, toward which they are living?*

CHAPTER 5

RECLAIMING OUR ANCESTRAL KNOWLEDGE AND WAYS: ABORIGINAL TEACHERS HONOURING CHILDREN, YOUTH, FAMILIES, ELDERS, AND COMMUNITIES AS RELATIONAL DECISION MAKERS

We ask you [Creator] to bless us
And to bless all of our family members
And the people in our communities
I think it's important to bring all of our people into our thoughts
And into our prayers
There are so many struggles amongst our people
And so many hardships
And there are good things too
(Word image composed from Sister Dorothy's prayer shared in a narrative inquiry circle on February 24, 2008)

I know the sacredness of the language
Because I am a speaker of the *Ojibway* language
– *kanadanon kitinaywenanan*: "Our languages are sacred"
There is a song we sing as *Anishinabe* people in our ceremonial gatherings that
     honours the spirit of our languages
I am reminded of the struggles we have teaching and passing on the language to the
     young people
Many people have been affected by that loss
One does not realize it until a child asks,
"Why did you not teach my language to your mother?"
(Word image composed from Florence's journal entry written on November 8, 2005)

Our *Mi'kmaq* and *Anishinabe* Elders Sister Dorothy and Florence, remind us that as we live our lives we embody all of our experiences with all of the

79

people, all of the family, community members, and Elders who shape us along the way. It is, as we carry each person, including experiences shaped and shared with them, from sadness to joy, from hard experiences to those of celebration that we will move forward in good ways. A central thread in the experiences of Aboriginal people is the loss of language. This loss continues to reverberate in the lives of individuals, families, and communities. Part of moving forward in good ways means attending to the uniqueness of each individual that is, embracing and honouring each individual for who she or he is becoming. As becoming is never static or finished one way to understand one another's becoming is through stories. Revealed through stories are the identity entanglements, the stories to live by, within, between, and across individuals, families, Elders, and communities (Chung & Clandinin, 2009; Greene, 1995; Huber, 2008; Huber, Graham, Murray Orr, & Reid, 2009; Miller, 1998; Paley, 1998; Vinz, 1997; Young, 2005b).

And, so, we begin in storied lives ...

Khea

I can't quit thinking about Robbie (pseudonym)
In a Grade 10 math course
It was November
Robbie came to the door and handed me his math text books
I asked
"Why?"
He said he was not coming any more
I was almost crying
"Why?" I asked
The administration told Robbie he'd missed
"More than enough days"
There's a rule around attendance and mid-term exams
Robbie would not be allowed
To write his mid-term exam

But
He was doing so well
It was a large class
30 plus students
When I was working with him
One-on-one
He'd say
"Miss, I understand it!
This is the first time ever that I understand it!"

"Please stick with it"
I begged

He said that when he was away from school
He was taking care of his children
While his girlfriend came to school
He said
"I can't leave my kids at home alone
So I'm just quitting now"

Even though this happened a few years ago
This is one of the most discouraging experiences
I have ever lived as a teacher
It broke my heart
I cried so much that day
(Word image composed from Khea's experiences storied in a narrative inquiry circle on
November 7, 2006)

The questions Khea raised in this earlier shared story were shaped through her relationship with Robbie, a student she worked alongside in a Grade 10 math course. As Khea later inquired into her story of Robbie she explained that she too, like Robbie, was new to the school that year. Although she was aware Robbie had missed some classes because he understood the math concepts, Khea was not thinking he would not complete the course. On the day Robbie handed Khea his math texts and explained why he would no longer be there, Khea learned of a school policy which she, at that point, had not known. As Khea simultaneously learned of this policy and of Robbie's leaving, she experienced deep anguish. Later, as she talked with colleagues about Robbie's leaving school Khea realized that, as a teacher at that school, she was required to report students who missed a certain number of days. In these conversations Khea learned that the reason for her reporting was so that the administration could prevent students from writing mid-term exams. This policy was, in part, shaped by the provincial ministry of education. Khea's teaching in this *Mi'kmaq* school in her home community was directly shaped by ministry of education policies.

Yet, as Khea's story shows, the stories she lives by as a teacher are not those of surveillance of, but support for, students. Both in her living of this experience and then a considerable time later as she storied it in our narrative inquiry circle, what happened to Robbie, a youth in Grade 10 and the father of two young children was, for Khea, profoundly nonsensical, profoundly unjust. As she storied her living of this experience Khea described that Robbie was not told he should quit school. What Robbie knew was that he would not leave his daughters at home alone as their mother and he attended school. In this way, he felt "caught between a rock and a hard place. He had no choice." Khea's sense of Robbie's lack of choice highlighted ways in which the intergenerational narrative reverberations of colonizing

Aboriginal people is still at work in some Aboriginal schools. In Khea's story we see continuing reverberations in the community and in the lives of children, youth, and families who are composing their lives in the school, in their families, and in the community. What happened in Robbie's life at school reverberated into his life at home, and what happened in Robbie's life at home reverberated in his life at school. Yet, even with these backward and forward reverberations, decision making was not attentive to either Robbie's voice or his life. Instead, decision making was held by the administration of the school and the ministry of education. This non-relational decision making had profound implications in Robbie's life and in the lives of his family.

Jennifer
In my practicum experience I felt a connection to a young girl
Rachel (pseudonym)
I am now dealing with the affects of that relationship

Rachel
Is a "ward" of CFS (Child and Family Services)
She will be moved to a different foster home
One day from today
I am not sure if Rachel has yet learned this news
When I saw her last
I think she did not yet know

In this move to another foster home
Rachel
Will not be able to stay at the school she was attending

I will always remember
Rachel
She was a hesitant girl
Beautiful but unsure of herself
She remained quiet

Rachel
Reminds me of so many people
Even myself

To me
Rachel
Represents the failure of two nations
To care for a child

Rachel
Is torn between two worlds
It seems there is no way of reconciling the two

The cycle of disconnection
Continues
For her
For her family
For the school
For the children
Who have touched
Rachel
Or who have been touched by her
(Word image composed from Jennifer's journal entry written on December 29, 2005)

The questions Jennifer raised in her earlier storying of her experience emerged from within a relationship with Rachel, a young girl Jennifer worked alongside over a year prior to writing about her in her journal. As Jennifer showed in her journal entry, Rachel was taken from her family, school, and community, a decision that indelibly shifted Rachel's life composition. When Jennifer and Rachel met, Rachel was composing her life as a "ward of Child and Family Services." Over time, as Jennifer attended to Rachel's life she learned that a move to another foster home, school, and community was being planned for Rachel. This was a decision in which Rachel had no voice. Jennifer struggled with the fact that Rachel did not yet know this information; she also wondered if Rachel's hesitancy, her quietness, was shaped by the increasing disconnection Rachel experienced as she was moved from one family, place, and school, to another family, place, and school as though these moves were inconsequential in Rachel's unfolding life. As Rachel lived in the space "between two worlds," that is, as she navigated the space shaped in the meeting of the intergenerational narrative reverberations of colonizing Aboriginal people in Canada and the less heard narratives of Aboriginal people, Jennifer articulated her despair with the "cycle of disconnection" shaping Rachel's life. Jennifer knew that this cycle continues to reverberate in the lives of many people of Aboriginal ancestry, including within her life. At the heart of Jennifer's journal entry are questions of what might have been different for Rachel had someone included her voice, her thoughts, in the decision making profoundly shaping her life?

Brenda Mary
Dear Journal
I am thinking about schooling
My oldest daughter moved back to our home reserve
Her daughter is doing good in school
Academically

My youngest daughter also moved
To another community

All her children were bumped up one grade

I am thinking about the transition that happens when our children
Move from one place
To another
And their children
Move
There are no connections
Between home and school
There are no parallels

So
Our children get lost
Between home life and school
I think if there was a good strong connection children would feel more comfortable
And do better
In school
(Word image composed from Brenda Mary's undated journal entry)

Brenda Mary's questions raised in her journal entry emerged from her experiences as a mother and grandmother, as she lives alongside her daughters and granddaughters as they move back to and away from Brenda Mary's home reserve. One transition which Brenda Mary storied, the move of her daughter and granddaughter back to their home reserve, was a "good" move for her granddaughter. As she connected the experiences of this granddaughter with her younger daughter's recent move away from their home reserve to another community, Brenda Mary puzzled over transitions between schools, homes, and communities.

Attending to the futures of her grandchildren led Brenda Mary to question the transitions children are expected to make as they move from one geographic location, home, and school to another geographic location, home, and school. Brenda Mary was concerned about what might happen to her grandchildren when they are not familiar with a new physical place, a new home or new school. She was also concerned about the transitions children are expected to make as they move from home to school and back again. As Brenda Mary attended to her feelings about how there are few, if any, connections or parallels between home and school, she wrote, that "our children get lost between home life and school." Brenda Mary was filled with a sense of urgency for stronger connections between home and school, connections that would attend to the need for children to feel comfortable in school. Highlighted within her storying of these experiences are Brenda Mary's understandings that children's feelings about themselves in the place of school are intimately connected with their success in school. School is then, much more than "academic success."

5.1. RELATIONAL DECISION MAKING AS SHAPING COUNTERSTORIES TO THE INTERGENERATIONAL NARRATIVE REVERBERATIONS OF COLONIZATION

We began this chapter with storied experiences of relationships with children and youth and of questions around tensions they can experience as they make home, familial, community, and school transitions. These questions included: Why do we do it this way? Who decides? Can't I think about what's best for my child? For Aboriginal children? As Khea, Jennifer, and Brenda Mary storied the experiences noted earlier, and as we collectively inquired into their stories, attentive to the intergenerational narrative reverberations of colonization made visible, it was their attentiveness to the particular life of a youth, Robbie; of a child, Rachel; and of a grandchild that we were first drawn. Their deep yearnings for something different in schools also turned our attention toward the counterstories to live by which they were composing. Across Khea's, Jennifer's, and Brenda Mary's earlier storied experiences the counterstories to live by around which they were threading new possible intergenerational narrative reverberations were focused on understanding children and youth as composing lives shaped by multiple contexts, that is, lives shaped through multiple relationships in places in and outside of school. This need for understanding the multiple places and relationships shaping the lives of children and youth as they enter into schools is, as shown in the earlier noted stories, vital in Aboriginal families and communities given the ways in which the narrative of colonization continues to reverberate in present lives.

For example, as we collectively inquired with Khea into the story she told of her experiences alongside Robbie, she described that in her thinking about him, again and again, something she wondered about was if Robbie's decision to quit school might have been connected with aspects of the history of his and Khea's *Mi'kmaq* community of Eskasoni. As she inquired with us into her earlier told story, Khea storied that when her dad was young he lost his father and because of this, he and Khea's uncles worked hard in the woods to feed the family. As she reflected on this shaping influence in her dad's life alongside Robbie's more present decision, Khea storied that an aspect of the history in their community is that it is important to the men that the women go to school. Khea said, "So, the women are dressed well and sent to school. I think Robbie reflects history: he quit school so that he could look after his children and his girlfriend could go to school." What

Khea's past and present connections subsequently raised for us were further questions about the importance of this history, of this knowledge of the community, being known in the school. If this history, if this knowledge, had been known in the school, might the ministry of education policy around missed days and the writing of mid-term and final exams, have been shifted as Robbie's story of childcare became known?

This thread of situating the care of children as a priority and as a counterstory pushing back at the intergenerational narrative reverberations shaped through the colonization of Aboriginal people is also central in Jennifer's story of Rachel. Jennifer, not unlike Khea, calls for a repositioning of the voices of children and youth in schools; they are each insisting that children's and youth's voices be encouraged and respected in all decision making. Jennifer is additionally insisting that children's voices be encouraged and respected as they interact with institutions other than schools, institutions such as social service agencies. As we collectively thought with Jennifer's stories of her experiences alongside Rachel, we saw Jennifer's composition of a counterstory to live by, a counterstory that pushes back against the dominant narrative of colonization that created residential schools and which continues to reverberate in Rachel's life through social service policies still unfolding in ways in which Aboriginal children continue to be removed from their families, homes, and communities. This need to be guided in schools, and in all institutional settings, by voices so commonly not heard, such as the voices of children and youth, is also a thread in the new possible intergenerational narrative reverberations imagined by Brenda Mary.

As a grandmother, Brenda Mary is calling for the voices of children and families to be heard in school. In her desire for children to feel comfortable in school, Brenda Mary highlighted the need for communication, a kind of communication that ensures children's home lives, their home relationships, and their knowledges of and senses of connection with people and places do not become diminished or taken away as they transition into school.

5.2. NEGOTIATING COUNTERSTORIES TO LIVE BY OF RECLAIMING OUR ANCESTRAL KNOWLEDGE AND WAYS

In our initial drafts of our book we separated these earlier three stories from the many experiences storied by Khea, Lucy, Lulu, Brenda Mary, Jennifer, and Jerri-Lynn of the significant place of family, Elders, and community in shaping their stories to live by. As we continued our inquiry into each of the three earlier stories we saw that one way Khea, Jennifer, and Brenda Mary responded to the intergenerational narrative reverberations of colonization which their storied experiences highlighted, was to imagine different ways forward. These different ways forward entailed composing counterstories to live by; counterstories in which the significant place of family, Elders, and community members opened up new possible intergenerational narrative reverberations for experiences lived in schools, homes, and communities. As we now attend to the following storied experiences we think with some of these counterstories to live by as a way to show new possible intergenerational narrative reverberations.

Lucy
I find forgiveness hard
Because of my mom
And watching how the residential school
Shaped her life
She was only 5 years old when she went there
I think it impacted her so much
She was so young
I think my mom has learned to accept what happened to her in the residential
    school
But she hasn't come out very well
She had it so rough
My siblings and I grew up with my mother feeling that way
She couldn't teach us our language because of the residential school
She has never
Since then
Spoken her language
The *Maliseet* language
And she didn't encourage us to learn *Maliseet* or *Mi'kmaq*, our dad's language

So for me
Forgiveness isn't about forgetting
My mom can't forget
What happened to her in the residential school never goes away
It's always there
In her body

Her body
Lived through those experiences
(Word image composed from Lucy's experiences storied in a narrative inquiry circle on
January 28, 2006)

As Lucy storied this experience she showed ways in which the impact of the residential school continues to reverberate in her mom's life. This reverberation also reverberates in Lucy's life as she presently struggles to learn *Mi'kmaq*, her dad's language, the language of the community where she was raised, and the language of the community where she is now raising her family and teaching. Lucy's mom has not forgotten, nor can she forget what she experienced in the residential school; she also ensured that Lucy grew up knowing these stories. The long-term harm experienced by Lucy's mom through the residential school has been part of Lucy's life for as far back as Lucy can remember. Today, Lucy's mom's stories of these experiences give Lucy strength and courage to not fall into a dominant social narrative of the need for the survivors of residential schools to "forgive, to forget, and to move on." Instead, Lucy draws upon her mom's stories of her residential school experiences to compose counterstories to live by, counterstories focused on becoming a fluent speaker, of her children being fluent speakers, and of encouraging the children whom she teaches to be proud of their *Mi'kmaq* language and culture.

As we continued thinking across the experiences storied of family, Elders, and the community, the following experience shared by Lucy shows one way she lives her life as a teacher composing stories to live by of wanting to contribute to or to give something back to her community. Attending to Lucy's storied experiences supported us to see an indelible link between Lucy's mom's life and the potential of new possible intergenerational narrative reverberations becoming threaded into the lives of the children who attend the *Mi'kmaq* school in Membertou because of the counterstories Lucy lives by:

Every year I do a photography project with the children in Grade Three
It's all about community
Connecting the children with their community
Past and present
We start the project by my showing a map of our community
[Membertou, Nova Scotia, Canada]
This map shows our community
When we were first moved here
From our original location at the water

The children are amazed when they see this map
Because there are only a few streets

Then
I take out my photographs of our community
Photos taken in my childhood years
I tell stories about what I remember
I tell the children about how our community did not have water or electricity when we were
relocated here

I do this project because
For me
It's about respect
Respecting the past of our people
Of our community

But
I also do it because I think children need to know stories of their history
They need to know that the government relocated our community
They need to know that when we were moved
We had no water and electricity
But
All of the non-*Mi'kmaq* neighborhoods had water and electricity
The children need to know that our ancestors didn't give up
There is a story that when we were first moved here there was a snow storm and the men in
    the community each got a shovel and walked side-by-side to clean the streets

The children need to know these stories so they can respect their parents and
    grandparents

I think children learn to respect themselves when they know the stories of
    generations who came before them
(Word image composed from Lucy's experiences storied in a narrative inquiry circle on
January 14, 2006)

In these counterstories which Lucy storied herself as gradually coming to live by she focused on the need for the current generation of *Mi'kmaq* children in Membertou to know the inequitable history of their ancestors, past experiences in which "our ancestors didn't give up." Not all aspects of this history are easy to know. Yet, without this knowledge Lucy believes that the generation of children whom she is raising and teaching will not fully know who they are as members of the *Mi'kmaq* community of Membertou and of the *Mi'kmaq* Nation. It is in knowing their history that Lucy believes this generation of children will learn to live by stories of respect for their ancestors and, in this way that they will simultaneously learn to respect themselves. In all of this, Lucy is teaching the children about the power and place of composing counterstories to live by so as to keep undoing the lingering narrative of colonizing Aboriginal people in Canada.

In addition, through her counterstories to live by Lucy is simultaneously shaping new possible intergenerational narrative reverberations in which children have opportunities to come to know themselves and the histories of

their ancestors in respectful ways as they interact with the Elders in the
community and engage in inquiries which honour their knowledge

Every year in our school
The children make gifts for ten Elders
For the ten oldest Elders in the community
We do this close to Christmas
What the children make as a gift to the Elders are wreaths
We go out of the city and into the woods and collect tips off the spruce trees
Then
We all come back to the school and the children are organized into multi-age
      groups
Each group makes one wreath
This tradition is called "*PestieŌwaŌltimk*"[1]
It means "Honouring the old ones"
It only takes a day to do it and it's a really beautiful day

After the wreaths are made
Each group of children walks to one Elder's home carrying the wreath they've
      made
They present it to the Elder

Another project I do at school is a social studies project
I ask the children to research our community
It is a community history project
I ask each child to go home and to research the date our community was moved to
      this present location
I also ask the children to ask why our community was moved
Each child has to talk with a parent or grandparent and discuss the changes our
      community has gone through over the years

Then
I ask each child to go to an Elder and to ask four questions of the Elder
Questions like
What did you do when you were my age?

Something I didn't take into consideration was that some of our Elders aren't
      originally from here
So we worked in class to reword some of the questions
So then we asked
What was it like in our community when you first came here?

It was a wonderful experience
All of the children
Except one
Brought back answers to the interview questions
I've done this project a few different ways over the years
But what I've noticed is that when the children are able to draw on their family
      stories

Or the stories of the Elders' lives
They like this kind of learning
They are much more engaged in this kind of learning
(Word image composed from Lucy's experiences storied in narrative inquiry circles on
October 10, 2006 & December 1, 2007)

As we inquired across Lucy's stories shared in this chapter, we were struck
by the ways in which the stories Lucy's mom lived by, stories in which she
did not hide her memories of her experiences in the residential school, were
shaping the counterstories Lucy was composing and living by as a mother,
teacher, and member of the community. In time, as we inquired into Jerri-
Lynn's stories we saw a similar family story shaping the counterstories Jerri-
Lynn was composing and living by.

Jerri-Lynn

I've got to be more faithful in journal writing
I haven't been that good lately
I kinda forget to do this

I'm so frustrated I don't even know how I'm going to make the meeting today
My mom has been on a 2-week bender
You think she would be tired of drinking
She's been doing it since we were kids
I'm sick of it
She drinks and ends up screwing up her job and loses everything she has

How many times does she have to lose things before she says it's enough?
(Word image composed from Jerri-Lynn's journal entry written on February 25, 2006)

Similar to Lucy, the stories Jerri-Lynn lives by have also been indelibly
shaped in relation with her mom. Jerri-Lynn's mom was also a residential
school survivor. This was a courageous story for Jerri-Lynn to share, not
only in her journal but out loud in the narrative inquiry circle with Brenda
Mary, Florence, Jennifer, and Mary and also later in a whole group
narrative inquiry circle. In her story Jerri-Lynn showed how the
intergenerational narrative reverberation of colonization was, at that time,
continuing to shape her mom's life. Because of Jerri-Lynn's relationship
with her mom, it was also shaping Jerri-Lynn's life. It was hard for Jerri-
Lynn to understand her mom's drinking, an aspect of her mom's life that
had been a source of pain and tension between them since Jerri-Lynn was a
child.

In her journal entry earlier noted Jerri-Lynn expressed her anger and
frustration with her mom for drinking and she wondered why her mom
continued to compose her life in this way. As Jerri-Lynn, and we, continued

to think with this life shaping experience in her life we grew in understanding that becoming angry with her mom was a way to understand how Jerri-Lynn, at times, fell into the intergenerational narrative reverberations of the colonization of Aboriginal people. Within the dominant narrative of colonizing Aboriginal people a central focus was to reshape Aboriginal children so they became ashamed of their parents. When Jerri-Lynn felt disappointment about her mom this dominant narrative continued to reverberate between her and her mom, just as we imagine the colonizers, past and present, desired. They knew that separating, tearing children away from their parents was a central way to reshape who the children would become.

Written between the lines of her journal entry and the emotions she expressed as she both read aloud and then later inquired into her story, were Jerri-Lynn's wishes for things to be different. Jerri-Lynn wished for her mom to be healthy and for her, her mom, and her mom's grandchildren, Jerri-Lynn's children, to have sustained relationships.

Jerri-Lynn's wish for renewed and healthy relationships within their family, similar to other Aboriginal families, did not happen.

My life has been changed
Forever
My mom passed away
How can my mom die?
How can I live the rest of my life without her?

I never got to spend much time with her over the past month or so
And now she is just gone
Gone
Forever
I love her with all of my heart

She is going to miss one of the most important parts of my life
She was always so happy I was going to school
She was so proud of me
She would always brag to her friends
"My girl is going to be a teacher"

Now
She won't even see me get there

How can she be gone?
My heart aches that she couldn't get over her problems
That she couldn't fight away her demons
My mom was one of the most important people in my life

Sure
We didn't have the greatest childhood
But I am grown up now and none of that matters anymore

I try so hard to remember her
Her voice
Her small lips
Her tiny hands
Her smile
Her snort when she laughed too hard

I never want to forget her

With all her battles she fought within
My mom was a sweet, kind-hearted woman
She cared deeply
For the ones she loved
And the kids she worked with
She was always there for me and my sister and our kids

Now she is gone
I didn't even get to say good bye

I talked with her the Friday before she passed away
She was drunk
She told me she was dying
I didn't believe her because she had said that so many times before
Over the years when she was drinking I didn't believe her
Why didn't I go check on her?
Maybe I could have helped her?
Maybe she would still be here?
I just hated seeing her when she was like that

My heart is so filled with what ifs
What if I went there?
What if I could have gone to AA with her?
What if I tried harder to help her stop drinking?
And so many more   ...

I don't want to live without her
I do not want to be without her
I love you Mom

It has been one month and 4 days exactly
I miss my mom so much
In everything I do or see
I think about my mom
I cry every day
I will be fine

Then
All of a sudden I will do or see something and then the reality that my mama is no
     longer here hits me
Maybe it's not as bad as it was

A couple of weeks ago when I would wake up
First thing in the morning I cried
Now I find it's at the end of the day when I go to bed

I absolutely know in my heart
That she is not here anymore
But I still find it really hard to believe

I don't feel like doing anything anymore
What's the point?
I'm going to school and learning all this stuff to one day die!

Sometimes it just seems so pointless

I wanted my mama here to watch me graduate
To see Raquelle, Dennis, and Andrew grow up
To see her great-grandchildren

How can she be gone so soon?
Why did this happen so fast?
There was so much more for her to do with her life
She was planning to go to Red River College to take applied counselling
She was supposed to start September 15th
She was supposed to be here for Christa and me and our kids
To share so many special moments that haven't even happened yet

Now Thanksgiving is coming up
She is not here
How will it be?
It was always our little family
Together
I don't think I am looking forward to it
I know we have to make new memories and move on
But how?

I just want her back
No matter how hard I ask
Wish
Beg
For her to come back
I know it won't happen
It's hard to believe that I have to live another 50 or more years without her

I miss you Mom
Soooo MUCH!!
(Word image composed from Jerri-Lynn's journal entries written
September 15 & October 8, 2008)

In the midst of Jerri-Lynn's pain which she storied in the two earlier noted journal entries, and then read aloud and further thought with in two subsequent narrative inquiry circles, her desires, her longing to be with her mom, her knowledge that she needs to have her mom in her life, and that her grandchildren also need her to be in their lives, showed us the counterstories to live by which Jerri-Lynn is slowly, agonizingly, coming to compose. Although Jerri-Lynn's composition and living of these counterstories cannot undo the devastation shaped in her mom's life because of her experiences in residential schools, they are a forward looking call for relational decision making. It is easy to imagine that if Jerri-Lynn's mom had grown up in a time when decisions for or about Aboriginal people were not made by others, she would likely never have found herself taken away from her parents, family, and community and enduring years of abuse in an Alberta residential school. The scars from these experiences reverberated across her entire, short life. These reverberations also shape Jerri-Lynn's life.

In time, as we narratively inquired into Jerri-Lynn's earlier storied experiences we saw a similar family story shaping the counterstories Brenda Mary was composing along side her daughter. In particular we noted Brenda Mary's composition of a counterstory to live by of supporting her daughter to restory, to figure out in new ways, the pain of not being able to speak her language.

Brenda Mary

I finished reading your book
Pimatisiwin, Walking in a Good Way (Young, 2005)
And will refer back to it several times in my lifetime as reference to read again
    and again
My daughter wanted to steal my copy of your book because when she read it she
    felt touched
I think she felt touched most likely in the part of her that does not know how to
    speak her language
She feels angry at whoever took it away
Meaning the system
She did not get that far as to say that
But I can fill in the missing blanks because I know her
She is my daughter
She said she would like to read your book in its entirety sometime
I told her she should talk to you sometime

She only has a Grade 5 level of education
She is upgrading herself right now twice a week
She realizes how important education is in today's world
My daughter wants to work in the field of medicine and she has an excellent
    memory for numbers
That is a start for her
(Word image composed from Brenda Mary's undated journal entry)

As Brenda Mary reflected on the powerful place Mary's book, *Pimatisiwin: Walking in a Good Way: A Narrative Inquiry Into Language as Identity* (2005b) had in her journey she told a story of her daughter. Wanting to steal Brenda Mary's copy of Mary's book, her daughter showed the deep connections she felt with Mary's stories, especially in relation with the ways in which Mary wrote about language as identity. It was in relation with this thread and the anger Brenda Mary's daughter expressed that we saw both the continuing intergenerational narrative reverberations of colonization through the loss of language, and therefore, identity, in both Brenda Mary's life and in the life of Brenda Mary's daughter. But, it was also in relation with this thread that we saw the counterstories to live by that Brenda Mary and her daughter were composing, counterstories to live by around new possible intergenerational narrative reverberations that look toward a future in which they are each becoming fluent in *Anishinabemowin*. Woven with their counterstories to live by is the significance of gaining strength from connecting with others, such as Mary, as part of a process of reconnecting with who they each are and who they are each becoming.

A second new possible intergenerational narrative reverberation is visible in the dream Brenda Mary's daughter holds for herself, a dream of "work[ing] in the field of medicine." Brenda Mary's support and encouragement of her daughter was deeply present in her story, expressed in her words: "That is a start for her." It is not difficult to imagine that in many places and relationships Brenda Mary's daughter's "Grade 5 level of education" would be not seen as shaping possibility but as a hopeless aspect of her life. Brenda Mary, however, encouraged her daughter to see that her learning journey can continue to grow long into the future. She believes in her daughter, and she tells her daughter that she believes she will reach her dream of working in the field of medicine.

As we continued to think with the stories shared of family, Elders, and the community, the following story shared by Brenda Mary, which tells of her own unfolding learning journey, helped us to see that similar to how she supported her daughter, Brenda Mary has drawn on the support of family. In the family relationship we recognized in Brenda Mary's stories we realized our need to show how central family is in supporting her to fulfill her dream of becoming a teacher.

> I shared a lot with my brother-in-law about the seven courses I am taking and
>   realizing how important my time is
> He told me I may want to reconsider taking the paying position because of the
>   importance of my time as a student
> Not to short change myself as a student
> What he was really saying was weigh the pros and cons to see if I can afford the
>   time
> I told him all my subjects are hard
> I want to develop a time management schedule for myself for my courses
> My brother-in-law told me to attend every day and every spare moment I have
>   to use it well
> If I have an hour to use it to do assignments
> When I come home take a rest
> A break
> If I need it
> Then
> Hit the books again
> Look how long it took me to realize how to manage time
> I started going to adult ed. back in 1997–98
> I heard people talk about it back then but I was not there yet to manage my time
> (Word image composed from Brenda Mary's journal entry written on October 20, 2006)

In her storying of this experience we saw Brenda Mary composing a counterstory not always common in all Aboriginal families given the devastation shaped by the residential schools. As she listened, and tried to compose her life in the ways her brother-in-law encouraged, Brenda Mary grew hopeful about sustaining her journey of becoming a teacher.

In the word image that follows, which we also composed from a journal entry Brenda Mary wrote in October 2006, Brenda Mary highlighted a "learning day" she experienced at a conference. During this day Brenda Mary learned about making a Star Blanket. She was excited to know about ways the Star Blanket "fits with math curriculum." Brenda Mary also, however, described the importance of her time with the woman who taught her about the Star Blanket. She valued this kind of learning, learning that happened outside her regular university classes. It is learning that comes to life as people sit side by side and share their knowing, their lives.

> Dear Journal
> It was a good day today
> I attended the "Circle of Knowledge and Practices" conference
> I learned about a star blanket
> How you can incorporate curriculum into such a project as making a star blanket
> I also gathered information on Star Blankets

How when you use strips of three you make a small size Star Blanket
The more strips you use the bigger the blanket
It fits with math curriculum as far as all the shapes go
There are diamond shapes, triangle shapes, squares, rectangles, and circles around
    the diamond patterns that make the eight pointed star
That was pretty neat
The woman gave me her name and phone number
She is willing to sit with me and my sisters or any group of people to teach us how
    to make a Star Blanket

I asked her a few questions about colors
"How many colors would you use?"
She said, "Three"
And fabric
"What kind of fabric would you use?"
"Overall how much would you need to spend on material?"
She said
"About $40 and your time would be a weekend"
Sometime I want to sit with this woman

There was a part of me that felt guilty for skipping class to be there
But I felt like I had a learning day nevertheless
(Word image composed from Brenda Mary's journal entry written on October 20, 2006)

We understood Brenda Mary's storying of this learning day, a day of
learning that happened outside of her university classes, as a way to
highlight the counterstories she is gradually composing and living by. These
learning days were filled with different ways of interacting and of knowing
than those she typically experienced in post-secondary classrooms; they were
days that filled Brenda Mary with excitement, passion, and hope for her
future life as a teacher.

In time, as we continued to think with Brenda Mary's earlier noted stories
we saw a similar counterstory in the stories Khea lived by. In Khea's
counterstory we saw her deep sense of responsibility and commitment to the
members of her community. It was in this way, too, by attending to Khea's
sense of responsibility and commitment to the members of her community,
that we saw her similar sense of responsibility and commitment to her
children as well as to the youth with whom she interacts as a teacher.

Khea

When I left my home I went to university to attend law school
But
I eventually left law school because early in the program I learned the only way I
    would be able to fight for Aboriginal rights would be to work in a context
    where I looked at policies in relation with Aboriginal people

Policy analysis was not what I wanted to do
I felt like I was wasting my time

This brought me to a time of self evaluation where I asked myself:
"Okay, do I want to continue on with this law program that I don't feel
    comfortable in or do I want to go home and put back into the community
    what I took out of it?"
That has always been important to me that if I take from my community I should
    put something back into it
So when I thought about my decision in that way I thought:
"Okay, I'm going to put back now"
If we take funding from our community so we can have post-secondary education then we
    have a responsibility to do well in our studies because when we receive funding we need to
    realize that our receiving funding probably means someone else in our community,
    somebody who is also very proud of who they are has had their funding request
Rejected

There is not enough money for everyone

Because the university was in a city quite a distance from my home community I
    experienced a disconnect with my birth community
I got caught up in the urban life
But at the same time
I missed the security I felt when I lived in my home community
Urban life never gave me a sense of security
When I realized this I started to think about my future children
I knew I did not want my future children to grow up in the city
I wanted them to grow up in my community
So they would feel the same security I did

This idea was central when I decided to become a teacher

As a teacher I think I have actually impacted a lot of other students
A lot of the former students whom I have taught in junior and senior high
Have gone back to our community when they finished a degree
They are using their degrees to give back to our community
(Word image composed from Khea's experiences storied in a narrative inquiry circle on
September 8, 2007)

Khea's storying of her awakenings to the importance of giving back to her
community began, as she showed earlier, as she experienced wonders and
tensions about what she was doing in a law program that she felt was not
contributing to her dream of "fight[ing] for Aboriginal rights." As Khea
awakened to this intergenerational narrative reverberation of colonizing
the education of Aboriginal people so that what they experienced was
not what they chose or desired but, instead, was a program already
predetermined by the institution, she saw that if she stayed in that law

program she was headed toward "policy analysis," something which she felt was a waste of her time. As Khea described, these tensions brought her "to a time of self-evaluation." In this process, Khea asked herself: "Okay, do I want to continue on with this law program that I don't feel comfortable in or do I want to go home and put back into the community what I took out of it?"

Reconnecting with this story to live by of giving back to her community supported Khea in making a number of life-changing decisions: she decided to not complete the law program, she decided to become a teacher, and as a teacher, she decided to live by stories in which she would encourage the youth with whom she worked to also live by stories of giving back to their community. Shifting her stories to live by in this way, Khea realized the disconnections she was experiencing from her "birth community." As she recognized the loss of security she felt living in an urban place she longed to return home. Part of Khea's shifting stories to live by connected with her sense of possibly wasting what little funding is available for Aboriginal students to attend post-secondary education if she stayed in a law program which she already felt was not meeting her needs.

In this way, Khea gradually awakened to another intergenerational narrative reverberation of colonization, that is, the limited funding for post-secondary education. In storying her awakening, Khea storied herself as gradually coming to think about her responsibilities to the people in her community, people who may also be applying for post-secondary funding, and people for whom an opportunity to attend post-secondary school was not available because of limited funding. Part of Khea's shift in her stories to live by was also connected with thoughts of herself as potentially becoming a parent in the future. She wanted her future children to know a sense of place like she had as a child growing up in Eskasoni, a sense of knowing a place so well that being there shapes feelings of security and through this, inner strength.

As we continued to think with the stories shared of family, Elders, and the community, the following experience storied by Khea, which tells of her passions for ensuring that her daughters are fluent *Mi'kmaq* speakers, showed another way she is continuing to compose stories to live by of giving back to the community. In composing these stories Khea is simultaneously living by counterstories that shape new possible intergenerational narrative reverberations in which the *Mi'kmaq* language is being revitalized. This revitalization is not only happening in school but, as well, in families and in the community.

My oldest daughter is more fluent with the *Mi'kmaq* language than my younger
    daughter
I was home with her for her first 2 months
And I only spoke *Mi'kmaq* with her
I felt strongly that *Mi'kmaq*
Should be her first language
Her babysitters also always only spoke *Mi'kmaq* with her
They were all fluent *Mi'kmaq* speakers
They would never have considered speaking English with her because their English
    is not strong
Mi'kmaq is so much the way of these women's lives
I do not think you would ever catch them speaking English to anyone
They are strong *Mi'kmaq* women

But my younger daughter is less fluent with *Mi'kmaq* because when she was born I was only
    able to spend 6 weeks with her before I went back to work
I was a working single mom
So my youngest daughter started going to a babysitter at a very young age

The babysitter always spoke English with my youngest daughter
She also took my daughter to her grandmother's house where all of the other
    children were speaking English
This really bothered me
When I came home I often caught the babysitter talking English with my daughter
She was saying things like
"Come here my little princess"
I was mortified when I heard English coming out of her mouth because words like
    "Princess" are not even part of the *Mi'kmaq* language

But I was also in a hard place because this babysitter was my only dependable
    sitter
When I asked her
"Why are you speaking to my daughter in English?"
She always started talking in *Mi'kmaq* with my daughter
I always told her that I did not want her to speak English with my daughter
But
Even though she is a fluent *Mi'kmaq* speaker she chose to speak with my daughter
    in English

My parents have also always spoken *Mi'kmaq* with my girls
They are both fluent *Mi'kmaq* speakers
But my daughters and their cousins always talk with each other in English

Two of my girls are in the *Mi'kmaq* immersion program at the school
They're both doing very well

Something my girls and I do at home when I'm doing the dishes at night
We talk in *Mi'kmaq* saying the months of the year, days of the week, and so
    on

I let my girls teach me because sometimes they know some of the words better
    than I do
They love this
I love this

Being with my girls and watching their growth as *Mi'kmaq* speakers has taught me
    so much about being a teacher
I teach math which can be a very linear kind of learning
Over the years I've noticed that a lot of youth have difficulty with the linear notions
    of some of the concepts
What I've learned is that if I translate the concepts into *Mi'kmaq* they understand
    them
This makes me think about how my maternal instinct doesn't stop with my girls
It's also with me as a teacher as I work with youth
Teaching is so much more than teaching the outcomes
As a mother and as a teacher
I try to always think about what more I can do
To support my girls
And the learning of all *Mi'kmaq* youth
As their lives unfold
(Word image composed from Khea's experiences storied in narrative inquiry circles on
November 19, 2005 & September 8, 2007)

In storying these experiences Khea showed how her living by a story of
giving back to her community has woven into the counterstories she lives by
as a mother and as a teacher. Khea showed her passions for the *Mi'kmaq*
language, a passion she instills and supports in her daughters, and also, that
she encourages in junior and senior high math classrooms. Unlike in her
earlier experiences in the law program in which her voice was not attended
to, in the counterstories she lives by as a teacher and as a mother, Khea is
not composing differing stories for these differing relationships. What she
wants for her children, she wants for all of the children in the community of
Eskasoni and the *Mi'kmaq* Nation.

As we continued to think across the stories told of family, Elders, and
community we saw Lulu living stories similar to those Khea was living by in
that who Lulu is as a mother is inextricably woven with who she is as a
teacher.

Lulu

One year when I was teaching the Grade 8 *Mi'kmaq* language course
The youth told me at the beginning they felt they had been
"Talked to death about basket making"
I said to them
"Is there anything you want to learn about your culture?"
They said they wanted to learn more about the history of our community

These young people's interest led us into a whole term of working with Elders
    from our community
The entire time I was a Grade 8 *Mi'kmaq* language teacher I worked with the Elders
Even before the Elders Centre was built in our community I would phone up all
    these Elders and say
"Are you available tomorrow afternoon from 1:00 pm to 3:00 pm?"
All these Elders came to the school
Some were even in wheelchairs
All I needed to do was call them the day before
They were amazing!
They brought photographs of their schools
Their classrooms
Their clothes
For the full 2 hours all of the Grade 8 youth
There were more than 60 of them in the classroom
They just sat there
Jotting down notes
Just listening
So closely
One time this one Elder
After the sharing
Pulled me aside and said
"What did you do with them? What did you do to them? Did you bribe them?"
When I saw how engaged the young people were I wondered if this was
Maybe the first time
They had a chance to be with Elders
To listen to their stories
To be able to ask the Elders questions
The biggest thing I noticed over the years we worked with the Elders was that the
    youth seemed to become prouder and prouder of who they are when they had this time
    with the Elders

Something else also happened ...

Last year, John (pseudonym)
One of the Grade 8 boys
Was looking at some of the photographs I've been able to pull together that show
    some of the history of our community
He was holding a photograph of some hockey players in his hand
He said
"Can I research this?"
His grandfather was in the photograph
I initially thought he was asking if he could do research on his grandfather
On his grandfather's history
Then, John said
"No, no, the hockey team. I want to do a history on them."

John went to this one Elder, Greg (pseudonym)

After the project was over John's dad stopped to tell me that he went with John to
    do the interview
They took Greg to the supermarket
Bought him supper
Spent the whole evening sitting in the upstairs part
Just talking
And laughing
John's dad told me it was the first time in 20 years that he'd seen Greg smile
Greg's wife passed away about 20 years ago
He was never the same after that
He just wore dark glasses
Drank tea and walked the streets of the community
Pretty soon lots of people in the community were saying that Greg seemed happier

I am coming to see that involving Elders in our school is good for both the youth
    and for the Elders
When John's dad told me this story about Greg
I thought to myself
"I wonder if Greg is happier because somebody took the time to connect with him
Took the time to hear his stories"

Earlier this year
Greg died
On the morning of the day he died John came to the classroom
He asked me
"Do you remember my project from last year?"
I said I did
John said
"You know what? Greg's dead. He died this morning"
Then he said
"I'm sure glad we have those tapes of his stories"

Ever since then I think about the healing that happens when Elders and youth can
    share their stories and learn together
John didn't really like school before we did that project
Greg seemed so sad and lonely before John interviewed him
I think they were both healed
By the relationship they made in the project

It was the youth who asked to learn about the history of our community
It was also a real process of learning for me
I started by trying to find information about the history of our community
Information we could read in class
I was very disappointed
I could only find two pages
I was shocked and asked myself
"Where's the rest? There's so much more history to our community"

John's project with Greg shows me that asking the youth to tell me what they
    wanted to learn was very powerful
It made me wish that our school board would do something similar with our
    community
We need to ask the parents of the children we teach what they want us to teach to
    their children when they are at school
We need to say to parents
"What do you want us to teach your child? What do you want your child to know?
Do you want us to teach the *Mi'kmaq* culture and language? Or, do you want us to teach
    about the Grand Council?"
Maybe a parent would say they want their child to learn to respect Elders
Then we need to keep asking
"What about you, what about you, you, and you?"

I think if we asked parents this question
Some would say
"Oh, I can help out with that
I know how to do that
I can help you because I can make that"
I think we need to begin with the parents
We need to have their input
Then once we know what the parents want
We need to go to the Elders to ask for their guidance
"How would we teach this? Is this the right way to teach this? How do we make
    this? Is this right?"

I think this kind of education
Would be about healing our people
Supporting our strength as a people

I remember this one time
When Rita Joe
Visited our classroom
She shared with the youth stories of her experiences in residential school
The youth had a hard time believing that Rita's stories were true
They were bawling and bawling
It was hard for them to hear the stories
But I think it's so important
That they know this part of our history
By knowing these stories
They will become stronger people
Which makes our communities
Stronger

As a teacher and as a parent
I was really happy to hear about something that happened last week
My daughter and oldest son are at the high school
And two Elders came to the school to interview the students

They wanted to hear the voices of high school students
What they thought about how our community is being governed
They told the students they are trying to change how our community is currently
    being governed
The Elders told the students they are going to choose some of the youth from the
    community to become members of the governance for our community
I was so happy when I heard this
And I thought
"That's the way it used to be a long time ago before we were colonized"
Our communities were governed by listening to all people's voices
It was important to hear voices from all ages
As this kind of new governance happens in our community
I think it will have a big impact on our schools
The provincial government is still too involved in our schools
Our schools need to be shaped by the voices of the students inside of them and
    by their parents and the people in our community
I think the ways the Elders are working for change in my community is so
    important
(Word image composed from Lulu's experiences storied in narrative inquiry circles on
November 19, 2005; October 10, 2006; November 7, 2006 & February 24, 2008)

In Lulu's storying and restorying of her experiences during many
narrative inquiry circles we grew in our understanding of ways in which
she, too, is composing counterstories to live by with potential to push back
against, and to interrupt the intergenerational narrative reverberations of
colonization. Similar to Jennifer, Lucy, Jerri-Lynn, Brenda Mary, and
Khea, Lulu's composition of counterstories to live by are intimately shaped
in relation with, that is, they emerge from within, her life experiences.

I know the sacredness of the language
Because I am a speaker of the *Ojibway* language
– *kanadanon kitinaywenanan*: "Our languages are sacred"
There is a song we sing as *Anishinabe* people in our ceremonial gatherings that
    honours the spirit of our languages
I am reminded of the struggles we have teaching and passing on the language to
    the young people
Many people have been affected by that loss
One does not realize it until a child asks,
"Why did you not teach my language to your mother?"
(Word image from Florence's journal entry written on November 8, 2005)

We ask you [Creator] to bless us
And to bless all of our family members
And the people in our communities
I think it's important to bring all of our people into our thoughts
And into our prayers
There are so many struggles amongst our people

And so many hardships
And there are good things too
(Word image composed from Sister Dorothy's prayer shared in a narrative inquiry circle on
February 24, 2008)

Who can deny that the intergenerational narrative reverberations of colonization have not shaped Brenda Mary's, Jennifer's, Jerri-Lynn's, Khea's, Lucy's, and Lulu's lives, past and present? In storying their lives they show this intergenerational shaping but, in their storying and restorying they also show additional aspects of their lives. In their living today, Jennifer, Lucy, Jerri-Lynn, Lulu, Brenda Mary, and Khea are composing stories to live by that seek to counter, to interrupt the harm done to them and to their ancestors. Jennifer's, Lucy's, Jerri-Lynn's, Lulu's, Brenda Mary's, and Khea's counterstories to live by are filled with possibilities for shaping new possible intergenerational narrative reverberations. Will you walk alongside Jennifer, Lucy, Jerri-Lynn, Lulu, Brenda Mary, and Khea? Will you become part of the cultural, familial, linguistic, institutional, and social restorying to which they are reaching, toward which they are living?

NOTE

1. As described in the *Mi'kmaw-English Lexicon: L'nui'sultinej*, "PestieÕwaÕltimk" is a noun which means "honouring ceremony" (Mi'kmaw Kina'matnewey, no publication date given, p. 30).

CHAPTER 6

BECOMING "REAL" ABORIGINAL TEACHERS: COUNTERSTORIES AS SHAPING NEW CURRICULUM MAKING POSSIBILITIES*

Our people have knowledge that has sustained us for thousands of years
Our ancestors went into the treaty making process after conducting many
   ceremonies.
They did this because they did not think of only the time being but for many
   generations ahead
They wanted to make sure that what they were doing was the right thing
(Word image composed from Florence's journal entry written on December 2, 2005)

What I learn today
What each of us learns today
Doesn't stay with us
It has to move out of us
It has to move elsewhere
It's like if you put a pebble in the water
We don't know where the ripples end, do we?
Imagine when that ripple effect comes into generations!
(Word image composed from Sister Dorothy's experiences storied in a narrative inquiry
circle on February 24, 2008)

Our *Anishinabe* and *Mi'kmaq* Elders, Florence and Sister Dorothy, remind us that the knowledge of Aboriginal people has been carried for many generations. This knowledge has been sustained through oral teachings and has survived for thousands of years; this knowledge continues to sustain Aboriginal people. The sustaining nature of this knowledge, of these oral traditions, has been shaped because of attention to the future, to

---

*An earlier version of this chapter was published in *Teachers and Teaching: Theory and Practice* (Taylor & Francis) in 2010.

the next generations. There are, then, responsibilities that come with knowing and learning from this oral knowledge. These responsibilities include sharing the stories of what we know to make a difference in the lives of people today and in the lives of people to come (Archibald, 2008; Cajete, 2001; Sarris, 1997).

And so, we begin in storied lives ...

Jerri-Lynn

It just makes me think of my own life up until now
Who ever thought I would be in university?
I always thought university is for "really smart people"
Surprisingly
To myself
I can do this!
I can be
A student
Mother
Sister
Daughter
A partner to someone

I think about the first time I went to the U of W (University of Winnipeg)
I remember when the ASSC (Aboriginal Student Services Centre)
Was in the basement of Bryce Hall
I went there and I thought
(I've never told anyone this. I don't want to offend anyone)
"Of course they put the Native people in the basement"
Then
When I went downstairs and I was greeted by the staff
They introduced themselves and helped me
Right away
I can't exactly think of how I got introduced to Mary
But
Eventually we were introduced
She was so helpful
I remember she was sitting down with me
Asking how I was going to pay for school
She was so helpful

She didn't look at me any different because I wasn't Aboriginal "looking"
I told her I was going through student loans
At that time I was a single mother on welfare
Maybe welfare would help me
She then told me about a really awesome bursary
For 5 years
All tuition and books would be paid for

Through Great West Life
It was for Aboriginal students
I was so excited
I jumped all over it
It only took less than a week to get all of the info I needed
Mary helped me with welfare
She and the Centre staff
Went as far as talking with my case worker to see if they would cover my cost of
    living
Needless to say they wouldn't
To make a long story short
I actually won the Great West Life (GWL) Aboriginal Access Award
I am so blessed
I couldn't believe it happened

I have two people to thank for where I am today
Mary, for encouraging me and telling me about the award
And GWL for helping me get my education
I am THANKFUL!!!
(Word image composed from Jerri-Lynn's journal entry written on April 11, 2006)

As we collectively inquired into the earlier experiences storied by Jerri-Lynn we were filled with many insights, questions, and tensions. Our attention was first turned toward the feelings of inadequacy Jerri-Lynn shared at the beginning of her story, feelings of not being smart enough, of not looking Aboriginal enough, of not being financially secure enough. As she entered a university landscape carrying these feelings Jerri-Lynn was not surprised by the marginal location of the Aboriginal Student Services Centre. Jerri-Lynn's feelings of inadequacy are significant as they are one way to trace the intergenerational narrative reverberations of colonization in her life. This impact occurred both prior to and during her journey to become a teacher, prior to and during the life journeys of her parents, of her grandparents, and back and back. Jerri-Lynn's storied experiences also highlight an experience resonating across her life and the lives of Brenda Mary, Jennifer, Khea, Lucy, and Lulu. This experience is of being excluded or silenced by dominant historical, institutional, and social narratives which position them as not *real* teachers as they become teachers, and researchers, in Canadian post-secondary places.

Thinking with Jerri-Lynn's storied experience attentive to the inter-generational narrative reverberations she makes visible, we saw at least two possible reverberations. The first reverberation, a reverberation maintaining the intergenerational narrative of colonization was that no person in Jerri-Lynn's immediate family had yet attended university. For Jerri-Lynn this meant that as she entered into a Canadian post-secondary place she did so with no familial or social narratives upon which to draw, no narratives that told her she could or would be successful in a post-secondary place. Woven into this reverberation were Jerri-Lynn's concerns about her physical appearance and the uncertainties she felt about being able to access the Aboriginal Student Services Centre, as well as potential financial support for Aboriginal students.

As we attended to this intergenerational narrative reverberation we saw that a second reverberation in Jerri-Lynn's storied life, a reverberation seeking to counter, to interrupt the lingering narrative of colonization and to start new possible intergenerational narrative reverberations, was shaped through the support of Mary and staff in the Centre who attended to the wholeness of Jerri-Lynn's life. In this place and these relationships Jerri-Lynn's desires to attend university to become a teacher and that, at that time, she was a single parent of two young children who needed financial support to be able to stay in school were taken seriously. In the Centre, Jerri-Lynn felt accepted for all of who she is, including her *Metís* ancestry and the particular needs of her life.

Jerri-Lynn's storied experiences show ways the Aboriginal Student Services Centre shaped new possible intergenerational narrative reverberations in her life. Through interactions with Mary and staff in the centre Jerri-Lynn's stories of needing food, a place to live, and childcare provisions were heard. As these aspects of her life were attended to Jerri-Lynn moved forward on her journey of becoming a teacher, a journey that, in time, supported her to live and tell new stories of herself, stories that she is capable of being in university and stories of being proud of her *Metís* ancestry. Jerri-Lynn's shifting stories to live by hold potential not only for shaping new possible intergenerational narrative reverberations in her life but, as well, in the future lives of her children, and in the lives of future generations of Aboriginal students as they enter into post-secondary places.

6.1. COMPOSING COUNTERSTORIES OF WHAT COULD BE "REAL" IN TEACHER EDUCATION AND LIFE IN SCHOOLS

There is much to think narratively about in the experiences storied by Lulu, Brenda Mary, Jennifer, Jerri-Lynn, Khea, and Lucy of ways their stories to live by rubbed up against narratives constructing them as not "real" teachers. Untangling these experiences shows ways the historically dominant narrative of colonizing Aboriginal people is still shaping intergenerational narrative reverberations, reverberations that weave into the life of each teacher, and as well, into the familial, communal, institutional, and broader provincial landscapes on which each teacher is composing her life.

Lulu

Teaching for 4 years
Still on term contract
But
Non-*Mi'kmaq* language teachers who started later than me
Have permanent contracts

A while ago
Feeling so tired
Wondered: "Why the hell am I here"
Tired of feeling
I needed to suck up to get a permanent contract
In the staff room a non-*Mi'kmaq* teacher with a permanent contract
Says we should go to the school board and lobby for three instead of one personal
    day per year
I was so angry when I heard that
"Who the fuck cares about personal days!"
Teachers on temporary contracts have no benefits
Like health care
Like pension
We lose financially
Our contracts expire every December
Every year we worry that contracts won't be renewed

The majority of temporary contract *Mi'kmaq* teachers wrote a letter to the school
    administration
We demanded better treatment
The main idea in our letter was that we want permanent
Not temporary
Contracts

I am really concerned because the majority of teachers with permanent contracts
    are not *Mi'kmaq* speakers
I keep asking: "How can teachers who are not *Mi'kmaq* speakers support children
    who are *Mi'kmaq* speakers?"
The children need fluent speakers to support them as *Mi'kmaq* speakers
Right?
And culture

I am so tired of being treated as an inadequate teacher
So tired of being treated like I'm not capable of knowing what to do

As a *Mi'kmaq* language teacher I do not have a classroom
That feels like I'm not
The language isn't
The program isn't
Valued
All of the other teachers have classrooms
They teach the government mandated subjects

But I fought for it
By voicing my voice
Today
The *Mi'kmaq* language teacher has a classroom
(Word image composed from Lulu's experiences storied in narrative inquiry circles on
November 7, 2006 & February 24, 2008)

Lulu's storied experiences reveal ways in which the dominant narrative of colonization is still reverberating in her community's school, shaping hiring practices where non-*Mi'kmaq* language teachers are offered permanent contracts while she and additional teachers of *Mi'kmaq* ancestry live tenuously, year by year, on term contracts. On her school landscape, Lulu experienced additional reverberations in her stories to live by that shaped, for her, further feelings of inadequacy as a teacher because unlike colleagues who taught the subject matter outcomes prescribed by the provincial government and who each had classrooms, as a teacher of the *Mi'kmaq* language, Lulu pushed a cart from one classroom to the next.

Lulu's stories show ways in which she and additional *Mi'kmaq* language teachers trapped in temporary contracts wrote a letter to the school administration, demanding contract equity. In their letter Lulu and her colleagues focused on the need for attention to identity in their school, that is, they focused on the need for understanding ways in which culture, language, and identity are intimately entangled. What they were asking their school administration to attend to was that in order to sustain the identities of the *Mi'kmaq* children and youth who attend the school, children and youth need to be able to learn alongside teachers who are *Mi'kmaq* speakers and who carry knowledge of the *Mi'kmaq* culture. Lulu and her colleagues saw these relationships as vital not only because of the ongoing loss of the *Mi'kmaq* language but, as well, because children now have the option to attend *Mi'kmaq* immersion classrooms from Grades Primary to 3. In addition, Lulu was insistent and vocal about the need for the junior high *Mi'kmaq* language teachers to also have classroom space. By the time this change happened, Lulu was no longer a *Mi'kmaq* language teacher but, still, she celebrated. She celebrated not for herself but for what the future might hold because of this shift, that is, new possible intergenerational narrative reverberations in which learning or maintaining *Mi'kmaq* language and culture in junior high is seen as important or "real" as subject matter outcomes mandated by the provincial government.

Brenda Mary

I struggle to think in these foreign ways
And in a language that is not my own

It does not come easy
I get lonely for my home land that I bonded with
I want to give up
Go home
For comfort
To people I am familiar with
Like my dad did when he finally came home
Broken
From residential school
My passion sends me to keep on
My family encourages me
To keep on
So I will keep on
I will make it a reality for myself and the ones who come here
To these college and university places
Behind me
(Word image composed from Brenda Mary's journal entry written on October 13, 2007)

Brenda Mary's storied experiences reveal ways in which the dominant narrative of colonization still seems to be reverberating in the institutional narratives she experienced, first in the context of a college and then in a university place. As she experienced both "foreign ways" of thinking and "a language that is not her own," Brenda Mary's stories to live by started to become reshaped by feelings of unfamiliarity and loneliness, reverberations which caused her to seriously consider giving up her dream of becoming a teacher.

As we thought with Brenda Mary's storied experiences we also saw that as a child growing up Brenda Mary came to know stories of how her dad was taken from his home community and forced into a residential school. As she came to know these stories of her dad's life Brenda Mary also came to know that her grandparents encouraged their son to come home because, in his generation, coming home meant hope for healing from the harmful effects of the residential school. At home, Brenda Mary's dad gained strength from his family. Yet now, in her generation, Brenda Mary knows that a new possible intergenerational narrative reverberation has begun in her family and community, a reverberation that means she cannot give up on becoming a teacher by going home. In this new possible intergenerational narrative reverberation in which Brenda Mary finds herself composing her life, she made her own choice to leave home to attend school. Brenda Mary's family's narratives are also shifting as family members, unlike in her dad's generation, encourage her to not come home just yet, but to complete her degree. Brenda Mary and her family are living by stories that look toward a future in which Brenda Mary's degree shapes new possible intergenerational narrative reverberations in their community through the kinds of experiences current and future generations of children, youth, and families will live in their community and school with Brenda Mary as a teacher.

Lucy

I sometimes hear non-*Mi'kmaq* teachers who teach in *Mi'kmaq* schools
Saying that because the teacher education program
I attended
Actively works to draw in Aboriginal students
It's not as "strong" as other teacher education programs
It's not as "strong" as other programs with student in-take
Based solely on marks

The story that we are "not as good" because we are *Mi'kmaq* teachers
Is causing problems in some Band schools
I think non-*Mi'kmaq* teachers are saying we are not as qualified
But they know we are and they're worried
Because each year
More *Mi'kmaq* teachers are graduating
I think non-*Mi'kmaq* teachers
Are becoming afraid of losing their jobs

Non-*Mi'kmaq* teachers in public schools
Feel somewhat similar
Local school boards want to hire *Mi'kmaq* teachers
This is causing hard feelings
In the public schools as well

For this reason I never want to teach in a public board
I think our colleagues would not support us
I don't know if parents would either

This also makes me think about how we
As teachers
Live with children
I tell the children they can call me by my first name

I think it's silly for children to call me Mrs. Joe
We live in this community
It's small and children from the community are always in my home
They play with my children
The children know me
As Lucy

This might seem like a small thing
But
It's not
When we call people by their names
It speaks to relationships
And knowing one another
This is so important in our schools
That the children feel they have
Relationships with their teachers
And that they know their teachers
And that their teachers know them
(Word image composed from Lucy's experiences storied in narrative inquiry circles on
January 28, 2006 & February 24, 2008)

Lucy's storied experiences reveal ways in which the dominant narrative of colonization still seems to be shaping intergenerational reverberations in the broader community. As she interacts with non-*Mi'kmaq* teachers who teach either at the *Mi'kmaq* school where Lucy teaches or in the public schools in the communities surrounding the *Mi'kmaq* community of Membertou, Lucy is told that the teacher education program she attended, a program consciously focused on the recruitment and retention of students of *Mi'kmaq* ancestry, is not "as strong." For Lucy, this narrative told of the teacher education program she attended shaped reverberations in her stories to live by of feeling "not as good" or "not as qualified" to be a teacher. In time, and as Lucy lived in the midst of these intergenerational narrative reverberations of colonization, she grew fearful of teaching in a public school, even though public school boards across the province are anxious to hire *Mi'kmaq* teachers. Lucy, however, fears she will be unsupported by both colleagues and parents of children in the public schools, the majority of whom are of non-*Mi'kmaq* ancestry.

While in her storying and restorying of her experiences, Lucy revealed that she did not think the tensions between *Mi'kmaq* and non-*Mi'kmaq* teachers and parents in public schools would shift in the near future, she did feel hopeful of a new possible intergenerational narrative reverberation, a reverberation shaped by increasing numbers of *Mi'kmaq* teachers who, each year, graduate from teacher education programs. Lucy is hopeful that as the numbers of teachers of *Mi'kmaq* ancestry in *Mi'kmaq* schools increase, and as future generations of *Mi'kmaq* children and youth experience success in *Mi'kmaq* schools and grow in pride as *Mi'kmaq* people, that the narratives told of *Mi'kmaq* people in the broader community will also shift.

Jennifer

My journey from childhood to today
Has taken many turns
I've encountered many dark stretches
I feel discriminated against by White people
And by Aboriginal people
For not fitting into either world

Yet these two worlds
Are not separate

I feel embarrassed for my attempts to embrace my cultural traditions
And for not knowing them to begin with

I feel different from some classmates
Who have seemingly "normal" families
And who do not know my hardships
Yet I do not feel bitter
Because I am proud of what I have overcome

Much of what I feel is contradictory
I haven't decided where I stand on certain issues regarding my identity
I feel stuck between two worlds
(Word image composed from Jennifer's journal entry written on October 29, 2005)

Jennifer's storied experiences made visible ways in which the dominant narrative of colonization still seems to be reverberating in the broader Canadian social context. As a person of *Anishinabe* and *Metís* ancestry Jennifer feels discriminated against by people of both Aboriginal and non-Aboriginal ancestries. Resulting from this discrimination, Jennifer experienced reverberations in her stories to live by of feeling that she does "not fit" in "either world." These feelings of not quite belonging continued to grow, reverberating into her family landscape as Jennifer, through interactions with non-Aboriginal students in university courses, began to feel that her family is not as "normal" as are her classmates' families.

A new possible intergenerational narrative reverberation revealed in Jennifer's stories is her understanding that the worlds, the lives of Aboriginal and non-Aboriginal peoples, are not separate. As Jennifer lives by this story of the need to understand these connections, she is working toward a future where cultural or racial hierarchies might be diminished and where future generations of children, of both Aboriginal and non-Aboriginal ancestry, do not feel the need to silence complex personal and familial histories and narratives. In these new possible intergenerational narrative reverberations future generations of children might draw upon their own and one another's complex narratives to shape fluid identities that are not "stuck" in-between "two worlds" but strengthened by participation in multiple and, at times, conflicting worlds and histories. In this way, they may be able to be "real" in both worlds.

Khea

When I applied to go to university
That was long ago
And things weren't so open
The university I first attended
Had affirmative action in place for a long time and across all faculties
But
As I studied there in the law program
I realized any program
And any university
That attracts Aboriginal students
The thinking out there
Is that students of Aboriginal ancestry
Can't be academic
So the thinking is that the program has lower standards
In this way not only does the program get labeled
But so can the university

You see what is happening here?
Programs that attend to Aboriginal students
Should be proud that Aboriginal perspectives
Are at the centre
But instead
The program gets shamed
Marginalized
(Word image composed from Khea's experiences storied in a narrative inquiry circle on January 28, 2006)

Khea's storied experiences turned our attention to ways in which the dominant narrative of colonization still seems to be reverberating in the broader provincial context where she lives. Even though the university she first attended as a student in a law program was shaped by policies of affirmative action Khea gradually realized these policies, meant to attract and support students of diverse backgrounds and experiences, were reinterpreted on the broader social landscape to mean that particular programs had "lower standards" and that the university, as well, was marginal. In other experiences storied by Khea she showed how she began to see ways this reinterpretation of affirmative action hindered students of Aboriginal ancestry when they applied for jobs. It was this realization that gradually shaped Khea's decision to not complete law school. The university where she subsequently engaged in teacher education did not, at that time, have affirmative action policies in place; it also does not actively seek to recruit or retain students of Aboriginal ancestry.

Khea's storied experiences revealed the continuing need for attention to accessibility in post-secondary places and, as well, in the hiring practices shaping the places where university graduates subsequently apply for jobs. While it is common for universities to gather data on the numbers of students who complete degrees, it is less common for universities to collect data on which particular graduates *are* hired. It seems vital for universities to know that accessibility may end the moment graduates complete their degrees. This knowledge could shape new and important conversations between universities and potential employers about ways of creating and sustaining equal opportunities in post-secondary contexts *and* in work-places. These conversations might also include participants from provincial and federal governments who set policy for Canadian employment and hiring practices. Canadian post-secondary institutions might also seek to shape reverberations of equitable hiring practices by encouraging each faculty to teach courses that include a focus on accessibility and equity as a way of restorying dominant institutional and social narratives. Attending to this kind of curriculum making as a responsibility of each faculty could shape the lives of future university graduates, people who leave university to undertake work in various fields with increased wakefulness to equitable opportunities, in their places of work and in the communities where they compose their lives. In these ways teachers and people who work in various professions might find spaces to stay attentive to the impact of their work, today and into the future, on the lives of current and future generations of Aboriginal and non-Aboriginal children, youth, adults, families, and communities.

6.2. IMAGINING CURRICULUM MAKING POSSIBILITIES

As we continued to collectively think with the stories of experience earlier shared in this chapter we initially co-authored a paper[1] in which we attended to ways in which Jerri-Lynn, Lulu, Brenda Mary, Jennifer, Lucy, and Khea were composing counterstories holding potential for pushing back against, for remaking dominant social, cultural, and institutional narratives which positioned them as not "real" teachers. By further attending to their composition of counterstories we began to see some of the new possible intergenerational narrative reverberations they were each reaching toward. Our co-authored paper concluded with our wonderings about the inextricable connections between counterstories and new possible intergenerational narrative reverberations. We were hopeful as we imagined ways in which wakefulness to these connections between counterstories and new possible intergenerational narrative reverberations could shape educative possibilities in the identities, in the lives, and in the meeting of the lives of Aboriginal and non-Aboriginal children, youth, families, teachers, and communities. However, as we published our paper, there was much we still wanted to think narratively about in relation with these stories, and the counterstories and new possible intergenerational reverberations which they inspired.

In this chapter we foreground one aspect of these earlier understandings which has long captured our imaginations: the curriculum making possibilities which become visible in the composition of counterstories focused on shaping new possible intergenerational narrative reverberations. As previously described in Chapter 1 our understandings of curriculum making are centrally attentive to experience, to lives in the making. Seven years ago as we began this narrative inquiry it was our interest in lives, and specifically, in the life curriculum making in which Jennifer, Lucy, Khea, Jerri-Lynn, Lulu, and Brenda Mary were each in the midst of composing as they navigated post-secondary places, which drew us to shape a tentative frame upon which we threaded experiential, narrative understandings of Aboriginal education, curriculum making, identity making, and place. Both then and now we see these experiential, narrative understandings as indelibly connected, as deeply entangled in the life writing, in the life curriculum making in which Lucy, Khea, Jerri-Lynn, Lulu, Brenda Mary, and Jennifer were, and remain, engaged.

From Chapter 1 readers are also aware that central within our understandings of curriculum making is Clandinin and Connelly's (1992) conceptualization of curriculum making as a "curriculum of life" (p. 392). However, seven years ago, our thinking in relation with this experiential, narrative understanding of curriculum making was centrally situated in school places, in post-secondary places. We now understand how curriculum making is "more than curriculum making in schools" (Huber et al.,

2011, p. 142). We now understand that "curriculum, at least the kind
that ... [speaks] of the lived experiences of making curricula of our
lives ... [are] also being made in homes and communities, with families and
others around diverse subject matters" (Huber et al., 2011, p. 142)[2] As we
now bring this more expansive, and more complex, understanding of
curriculum making alongside our earlier understandings of the composition
of counterstories which seek to shape new possible intergenerational
narrative reverberations we see how much attending to lives matters. We
also see how much is at stake and how vital this kind of narrative attending,
thinking, and living is: Who we each are and who we each are becoming is
continuously shaped and reshaped in this kind of life curriculum making. As
we return to each teacher's storied experiences to imagine what might be in
curriculum making in post-secondary places if we took seriously, if we acted
upon, the counterstories and new possible intergenerational narrative
reverberations toward which Brenda Mary, Jennifer, Lucy, Khea, Jerri-
Lynn, and Lulu are each reaching, many possibilities emerge.

6.3. BEADING SOME POST-SECONDARY
CURRICULUM MAKING WONDERS

One aspect of the lives of Jennifer, Lucy, Khea, Jerri-Lynn, Lulu, and
Brenda Mary that becomes visible in the first parts of this chapter is that too
often in post-secondary places students are only attended to in relation with
their "success" with the subject matters which dominate in courses. Yet, in
differing ways, Lucy's, Khea's, Jerri-Lynn's, Lulu's, Brenda Mary's, and
Jennifer's storied lives reveal ways in which attentiveness to their whole lives
mattered. If we imagine attentiveness to the whole lives of Aboriginal post-
secondary students we see that post-secondary curriculum making, like
school curriculum making, also needs to attend to the experiences, to the
lives students are composing in and with members of their home and
community places. We imagine then, that in this attentiveness to the whole
lives of Aboriginal post-secondary students that post-secondary curriculum
making would necessarily become much less dominated by the subject
matter knowledge held by the instructor. We also imagine significant
interaction between the diverse knowledge carried by Aboriginal post-
secondary students via the multiplicity of their experiences both in and
outside post-secondary places. In the current curriculum making of post-
secondary places this kind of curriculum making, curriculum making in

which the life of an instructor meets with the life of a student, usually only happens when a student is defined as "unsuccessful" and is then called to meet with an instructor to explain their "failure" in relation with the subject matter of the course. If post-secondary curriculum making became attentive to the whole lives of Aboriginal post-secondary students we imagine the opening up of new ways of understanding success, of the negotiation of much more complex knowledge, and also, that the ways of being for Aboriginal post-secondary students, and for faculty members, would also shift.

Another interwoven aspect that becomes visible in the earlier storied lives of Khea, Jerri-Lynn, Lulu, Brenda Mary, Jennifer, and Lucy is the need for much more attention to the deep connections among language, culture, and identity, and also, of the need for these understandings to infuse all aspects of the subject matters, assignments, representations of knowledge, and so on, in post-secondary classrooms. While attentiveness to these understandings in post-secondary curriculum making would likely continue to create much complexity, and tension, in post-secondary classrooms we also imagine that instructors would feel much greater uncertainty, feelings, too, that could open up greater negotiation among students and instructors in all matters of post-secondary curriculum making. Living in these ways would also likely, at least at times, shape conflict and tension in the meeting of the lives of Aboriginal post-secondary students and instructors, and in the meeting of all of the lives which meet in post-secondary classrooms. We imagine that in the midst of this tension-filled meeting of lives there would need to be much more openness to inquiry, and to change, change that begins with and within each person individually and, in time, that reverberates into new relationships and concerns among students with one another, between instructors and students, and with members of diverse communities outside of post-secondary places.

While the imaginings for post-secondary curriculum making which we have already beaded in this section are substantial, there is one more we wonder about. What might happen in post-secondary places if we became intentional about curriculum making which is wakeful to the inequitable hiring practices which many Aboriginal students face as they complete post-secondary education? In moving forward in post-secondary curriculum making in ways that are intentionally attentive to this lived experience, we imagine that a central consideration might be to explore ways for Aboriginal post-secondary students to connect with future employers while they are in the midst of their post-secondary journeys. While many post-secondary places already encourage various kinds of service learning in their curriculum making, might there be ways in which connections with future employees could be grounded less within an Aboriginal post-secondary student "serving" a community to which she or he might have little relationship and more about shaping new forward looking stories in the professions as a result of relationships, relationships which are nurtured and grow across the post-secondary years? Might this attentiveness to relationships also open up ways for Aboriginal post-secondary student to give back to their communities and to find ways of supporting next generations, two passions which, in both similar and differing ways, Khea, Jerri-Lynn, Lulu, Brenda Mary, Jennifer, and Lucy each highlighted as significant in their life curriculum making? We wonder.

> What I learn today
> What each of us learns today
> Doesn't stay with us
> It has to move out of us
> It has to move elsewhere
> It's like if you put a pebble in the water
> We don't know where the ripples end, do we?
> Imagine when that ripple effect comes into generations!
> (Word image composed from Sister Dorothy's experiences storied in a narrative inquiry circle on February 24, 2008)

> Our people have knowledge that has sustained us for thousands of years
> Our ancestors went into the treaty making process after conducting many
>   ceremonies
> They did this because they did not think of only the time being but for many
>   generations ahead
> They wanted to make sure that what they were doing was the right thing
> (Word image composed from Florence's journal entry written on December 2, 2005)

Who can deny that the intergenerational narrative reverberations of colonization have not shaped Brenda Mary's, Jennifer's, Jerri-Lynn's, Khea's, Lucy's, and Lulu's lives, past and present? In storying their lives they show this intergenerational shaping but, in their storying and restorying they also show additional aspects of their lives. In their living, today, Jennifer, Lucy, Jerri-Lynn, Lulu, Brenda Mary, and Khea are composing stories to live by that seek to counter, to interrupt the harm done to them and to their ancestors. Jennifer's, Lucy's, Jerri-Lynn's, Lulu's, Brenda Mary's, and Khea's counter stories to live by are filled with possibilities for shaping new possible intergenerational narrative reverberations. Will you walk alongside Jennifer, Lucy, Jerri-Lynn, Lulu, Brenda Mary, and Khea? Will you become part of the cultural, familial, linguistic, institutional, and social restorying to which they are reaching, toward which they are living?

NOTES

1. Some of the first parts of this chapter were previously published in an article in *Teachers and Teaching: Theory and Practice*. Please see Young et al. (2010).

2. As Huber et al. (2011) wrote of the ways in which their earlier understandings of curriculum making were interrupted, that is, ways in which they reconceptualized curriculum making to include the curriculum making in which children were engaged "alongside members of their families and communities in home and community places" they wrote:

> As we developed our reconceptualization of curriculum making, we wanted to understand ways children negotiate and navigate their unfolding understandings of themselves in their homes, communities, and schools and, as well, their experiences as they move within the spaces between these three, sometimes quite different, contexts. Our reimagining of curriculum making is threaded by our desire to restory the dominant social, cultural, linguistic, familial, and institutional narratives. These dominant narratives privilege teachers, other professionals, and policy makers as curriculum makers; however they also privilege school curriculum making over what we now see as the making of curriculum relationally composed in children's home and community places. (p. 2)

ACKNOWLEDGMENT

An earlier version of this chapter was published in *Teachers and Teaching: Theory and Practice* (Taylor & Francis) in 2010.

CHAPTER 7

BEING INCLUDED IN AND BALANCING THE COMPLEXITIES OF BECOMING AN ABORIGINAL TEACHER

For many years in my life after the Residential School I didn't think our language
    was important
So I did not speak it
In those years, too, I was teaching in a location far away from our people and
    language
But when I came home to visit, my father would say,
"Okay, you're home now, you speak the language now"
I would start to cry then because I wasn't fluent anymore and I'd say to him,
"Just give me a few days and I'll get it back"
But really I didn't think it was important because of the hardship it gave me
My language gave me hardship when I was at the Residential School and it gave
    me hardship when I came back home
I wouldn't speak at home and my father threatened to punish me
I think at that time I felt that my language had hurt me so much
But when my father died I just kept thinking
"I've got to keep my father alive. How do I keep my father alive?"
Then I realized that my father, and my mother, had given me a legacy
My language
That was 1974
That's when I became born again *Mi'kmaq*
I wanted to continue living everything my father valued
He was so proud to be *Mi'kmaq*
He was so proud of the *Mi'kmaq* language
He was so proud of the traditions
He was so proud of everything about who we are as *Mi'kmaq*
(Word image composed from Sister Dorothy's experiences storied in a narrative inquiry
circle on January 28, 2006)

It's hard to imagine what the communities and our homes were like without us
    children
It must have been so lonely

Even today
Anyone who has family misses family when they are not together
I remember the times we would be preparing to leave for school
My Mom and Dad would go to bed without saying goodbye to us or even giving us
     a hug
They could not face us leaving for school
Oh what pain they must have endured, too
All in the name of us getting civilized
I cry as I remember and write this
I wonder how many other households went through the same thing
We know what we want our First Nations students to learn
We all agree that respect is one of the foundations of what defines our values of our
     people
There are so many excellent teachings we can draw from
The hard work of collecting and doing the research based in the traditional
     teachings as the Elders have given us has really paid off
(Word image composed from Florence's journal entries written on May 1 & May 3, 2006)

Our *Mi'kmaq* and *Anishinabe* Elders, Sister Dorothy and Florence, remind us of the centrality of family in our lives and who we are becoming. When children are taken away from their families and familial contexts the suffering endured by the children, parents, family members, and community is unbearable. This removal of Aboriginal children from families, communities, and the places they knew was unnecessary. Aboriginal people have always known what they want for their children: "*We all agree that respect is one of the foundations of what defines our values of our people.*" This teaching of respect given to us by the Elders has sustained us in the past and in the present. These teachings will continue to sustain us into the future. The stories of our parents have sustained us too. When our mothers and fathers urged us to not lose our languages they were reminding us of who we are and where we come from. In this way they were giving us a legacy of being proud of our language, of our traditions, and of our ways of being Aboriginal people. It is as we claim and reconnect with these stories of the Elders and our ancestors that we know ways forward (Archibald, 2008; Cajete, 2001; Restoule, 2000).

And, so, we begin in storied lives ...

Jerri-Lynn

I'm pretty sure I will be taking spring/summer session this year
Maybe it will make my school go a little faster
I just can't wait to be a teacher

In our curriculum class we are doing course outlines
Yearly, monthly, weekly, daily plans

I Never really realized how much work went into being a teacher
Near the end of April our class will present our lessons
Hopefully it won't be too nerve wracking
At the end of this year we have to declare our majors
I guess I should make an appointment to find out

I am in class right now
I had the craziest weekend ever
Friday the kids and I went to my friend's for supper
Then on Saturday we took my Grandma, Aunt, and her granddaughter shopping
Then I went to my Aunt's house and de-liced her hair. It felt like forever to do it
Sunday we went to another's friend's for her daughter's 5th birthday
Ahhhhh—it was so crazy
I didn't have any time to do all my housework
Tomorrow is our first Intro to *Cree* test and I don't think I will get 100% but I think
    I will do well
School is still a little shaky. People are still talking behind other's backs. WHY
    CAN'T EVERYONE JUST GET ALONG? I keep saying, "We are all here for
    the same reason"

Yesterday we had our first research meeting. I was so excited to see what this
    whole thing was about. It will be neat to see how we all grow within this
    experience and the new relationships that will form from it

Back to school tomorrow
Had a crazy weekend
I did too much running around with the kids, my sister, and niece
I don't know if I'll go [to class] in the morning
Dennis' class (nursery) is having a Halloween party
Families are encouraged to go
I already missed the Thanksgiving get together
I don't want to be one of those parents who aren't there for their kids
Maybe I'm just trying to justify myself so I can miss class
We'll see how things go in the morning then decide
Just got Andrew to bed, better work on Dennis now
He'll probably need a snack, then clean teeth, a hug, a kiss, bathroom break, and
    then he'll find something else so he can stay awake
I better get my butt in gear. It takes time. Then gotta get cracking on the good ol'
    homework

Was late for school today
Just couldn't get my butt out of bed
It seemed like so much work to get the boys up. Make lunches and get everyone off
    to school and daycare
Dennis was 15 minutes late for school and I missed my first class
Thank goodness today is Friday
I think I need to start going to bed earlier and getting up earlier

It was a good day at school today
I learned a lot of new things in our Seminars on Aboriginal Topics class
We learned about the Royal Proclamation[1] and the White paper which Trudeau
    tried to introduce
I think I need to research them a little more because I don't know a whole lot about
    them
In our last Seminars class we watched a video called "Keepers of the Fire"
It showcased Aboriginal women who made a difference in the Aboriginal
    communities across Canada
It was really good
It showed the Elder women of the *Haida* Nation who took front line to stop
    deforestation on Lyle Island
And Sandra Lovelace who helped get Bill C-31
And the women who took the front line in Oka
It was amazing to see these women take a stand for their people
I'm also getting a better grasp of my *Cree*
I can spell better now and am picking up on words I had trouble memorizing before

My dad and step mom came in from Thunder Bay yesterday so I'll be spending
    some time with them this weekend
Tomorrow is my Grandma's 86th birthday
Wow, 86 years
My grandma's probably seen a lot of things in that time
We'll probably go visit for a bit with her tomorrow night, maybe dinner or
    something
Tomorrow will be our first meeting in the new year
I'm excited to see what my other comrades have been up to
It will be nice to see everyone tomorrow

I had an okay week
I didn't have very many classes this week
One of our teachers had an appointment
The other teachers had PD days
I'm almost done working on my lesson plans
It sure is a lot of work to do them
I'm going to my friend's tonight to type them out
I can't wait to get my own computer
It will make my life much easier with school
I can't believe that in just over 2 months I'll be done my second year of school
(Word image composed from Jerri-Lynn's journal entries written on October 13 & 30, 2005;
November 14, 2005; January 13 & 24, 2006; & February 5, 2006)

As we attended to Jerri-Lynn's storied experiences over this span of
5 months the richness and complexity of her life as she was becoming a
teacher were strongly visible. As she showed in her earlier shared journal
entries, as she lived in the midst of becoming a teacher Jerri-Lynn was also
living in the midst of being a mother to two young children, of being a

daughter, granddaughter, niece, and friend. Each of these stories to live by shaped multiple responsibilities in Jerri-Lynn's life. As a student in a teacher education program, Jerri-Lynn took seriously the work expected of her. She also took seriously the context of her program in which there were tensions among students, tensions which Jerri-Lynn tried to make sense of and to work on, together, with peers in the program. As a parent, Jerri-Lynn carried responsibilities for being alongside her young sons both at home and in their experiences at school. It was not easy to attend school full-time and to be a mother. At times, Jerri-Lynn needed to make choices between attending classes or being with her sons, such as at the Halloween party for one of her sons. As well, Jerri-Lynn simultaneously lived by stories of being responsible and present within her larger familial context as, for example, she spent time with her grandmother, father, step-mother, aunts, and nieces.

For Jerri-Lynn, being included in her journey of becoming a teacher necessarily entailed attending to these multiple stories she lives by. As we attended to Jerri-Lynn's life we saw that the balancing she negotiated each day was both very complex and very fragile. As Jerri-Lynn storied, some days she felt she lost balance and both she and her sons were late for school. While there never seemed to be enough hours in Jerri-Lynn's days she also showed how not having access to particular resources further shaped her feelings in relation with being included and of being able to balance all of the aspects shaping her life as she was becoming a teacher. For example, because she was not able to access a home computer Jerri-Lynn spent time at a friend's home using her computer to type up the lesson plans she needed to have ready for one of her courses.

As we thought with these storied experiences in Jerri-Lynn's life, attentive to intergenerational narrative reverberations we saw that there seemed to be no spaces in the teacher education program where Jerri-Lynn could make sense of her becoming in the midst of the multiplicity of her life. Indeed, twice over the span of the months as the earlier journal entries were written and shared, Jerri-Lynn reflected on how her participation in our narrative inquiry was shaping a space where she felt included in her becoming as a teacher. Our narrative inquiry was a space Jerri-Lynn storied feeling comfortable and where meaningful relationships were forming with all of the other women in the narrative inquiry circles. Similar to Jerri-Lynn's excitement in relation with the *Keepers of the Fire* (Welsh, 1994) and the lives of the women portrayed, Jerri-Lynn recognized the strength of Aboriginal women, both those with whom she participated in this narrative inquiry and those working for change in Aboriginal communities across Canada.

Thinking in these ways with Jerri-Lynn's storied experiences supported us to see that an intergenerational narrative reverberation that seemed to linger in the shaping of most post-secondary places is that becoming "educated" involves serious study of the knowledge passed from a professor to a student. In this kind of education there is a need to keep up with the assignments, a keeping up that does not always respect the multiplicity, and therefore, complexity of the lives of post-secondary students. It was in not losing sight of the multiplicity of her life that the stories Jerri-Lynn lives by, stories to live by of also being respectful and responsible with her children and extended family, that she is composing new possible intergenerational narrative reverberations. These new possible intergenerational narrative reverberations show new ways of living as a post-secondary student, ways that hold much potential for reshaping the dominant institutional narratives of post-secondary places.

Lucy

"We have each other""We have each other"
That's what I always say when people ask me how I'm experiencing the graduate
    program
"We have each other"
It means a lot to me that I am not the only *Mi'kmaq* student in the classes
It is sometimes really hard when we need to go to class in the summer
Especially when courses start on a holiday and I just want to have this day with my
    family
Sometimes during the fall and winter it's also hard
We need to leave so early in the morning to get to week-end classes on campus

In some of the courses
I feel like the professors are standing at the front of the room
Talking at me all day long, just telling me all this stuff
When this happens I never understand what they're teaching about because I
    haven't experienced it
I need to experience it
When professors just keep talking about their own experiences and how they
    received their doctorate
I just shut down
In my head I'm usually thinking: "Who cares?"
I always feel like my head is spinning

In a lot of courses I feel like you need to read the fine print
I don't think *Mi'kmaq* people learn that way
What seems to happen so much is that students are expected to learn for themselves
Mostly by writing papers
I dread that

Really, it's this aspect
So much focus on written work that made me change my mind about doing a thesis
I don't like writing papers
That's why I never really enjoyed school because I hated to write down my
      thoughts
I find it difficult
I like the oral thing
I like talking rather than just writing
I prefer talking to writing
I have decided I do not want to be like most professors
I don't want to be so self absorbed with who I am
With my work
I don't want to stand in front of a class and preach to 90 other people about how I
      did this research
And that research
I'm not like that
I don't want to be that person and I never have
So this is as far as I'm going with post-secondary
I have no desire to go any further if it means I have to become like that
I'm pretty satisfied with who I am and I just don't like what the courses have
      made me feel like or what they are trying to make me become
I feel like I just did not fit with most of the courses and all the stuff about how to
      do a proposal and a thesis
There were three professors in this one course on writing research proposals
I think their co-teaching didn't work
Instead of one professor talking about one thing and the next talking about
      another thing
It seemed like they each had to say something about everything
So they did a lot of talking
I think they each would have been great separately but they weren't good together
They all had their own different ideas of what a thesis should look like and how to
      do research
That's why my head was spinning
I got confused because I was trying to make sense of their different opinions
That really turned me off the whole course and the idea of doing a thesis

Now that I've had some time to reflect on that course
I realize that I just don't fit into the way those professors acted
I also don't fit with how some of the students acted
So many of the students only care about the mark at the end
Some students got upset if my mark was higher than their marks
Those students seemed to change themselves so that the professor would give them
      high marks
They would type everything and hand in way more than the professor asked for
I just can't do that
I don't want to change myself for a mark
Even if I wanted to I don't know how to hand in more pages
I don't know how to say the same things 20 different ways

That's what most professors want
I always felt like I was at the sidelines
Just watching things unfold

In the course where I made these decisions
All of the *Mi'kmaq* students sat apart at the edge of the classroom
By the time we drove a number of hours to arrive on campus there was no room
    in the classroom
Except at the edges

Another reason why I think I lost my confidence is that all of the *Mi'kmaq*
    students
Except me
Were placed into one group focused on language research
I wanted to focus on technology so I went to another group
But the whole time I felt that because I was a *Mi'kmaq* teacher
The professors really wanted me to focus on language

I brought this artifact to share in our research conversation tonight
A poster sent out to Nova Scotia schools each fall because October is "*Mi'kmaq*
    History Month"
The poster shows a bit about the history of *Mi'kmaq* people and our celebration of
    "Treaty Day" every October 1st[2]
I recently shared this poster in one of my graduate classes as a way to talk about
    curriculum and values
When I was sharing in the graduate class
I realized that this poster relates to what I experience
Think
And talk about
Every day as I work with *Mi'kmaq* children
When I was a child attending a public elementary school
Mi'kmaq history was never taught to me
Whatsoever
Instead
I was taught a blur of facts about how Columbus discovered America
In the text books we read there was always a sentence about "savages" but never
    the fact that Aboriginal people lived here first
We never learned anything about the *Mi'kmaq* people or the *Ojibway* or about
    Passamaquoddy[3]
None of these facts were ever mentioned
Because of this
My identity was pretty much taken away from me in school
As a child in the public school system all I ever knew about myself was that my
    ancestors were "savages"
And that I was an Indian girl living on a *Mi'kmaq* reservation in Nova Scotia

When I look at this poster today I just think about how different my experiences
    might have been
As a child

If the history shown here [motions to the poster]
Had been in my classroom
It makes me realize how much teachers teach their values
How teachers put their values onto students and try to make students be who
    teachers want them to be
I don't like that
I don't want to be that way as a teacher
I know it's hard not to teach your values
I know it's sometimes hard to let children be who they want to be

As a *Mi'kmaq* person and teacher
I think it's important that I am teaching children of *Mi'kmaq* ancestry because our
    values are related

I often wonder if I were to teach in the public school system and to show my values
    with non-*Mi'kmaq* students
How many calls would I get after school telling me that I should not be teaching
    their child about *Mi'kmaq* people
Or showing my *Mi'kmaq* values?
Yet that is what happened to me as a child
I was expected to live by the values of a non-*Mi'kmaq* teacher

I know the system has changed a bit since I was a child but I get tired of how
Once a year
In the month of October
All these government people
And other people
Want to shake hands with *Mi'kmaq* people
It's the same as how
Once a year
In the month of January
All these government people
And other people
Want to shake hands with people of African Nova Scotian ancestry
But, really, this is like a slap in the face
It's like we only care about you
And where you come from
During one month of the year
And other than that
We don't want to know you
Or where you come from

That doesn't make me feel very cared about
Not in a real way
This year
Because my oldest child is in a public school
He had to go to school that day [on Treaty Day, October 1st]
If we really value Treaty Day in this province then I think all of the public

institutions should be closed
Similar to how they are closed for Victoria Day in May

I wonder if we will ever live in a time when all of Canada's peoples
Celebrate National Aboriginal Day on June 21st

When I was thinking about what I could say about this poster in the graduate class
I knew I wanted to talk about how my experiences as a child in school
Are still at work today
The values that the non-*Mi'kmaq* teachers tried to brainwash me with
Are still being taught in the public schools today
Not all of the children in our community attend the Band school and the children
    who do attend the Band school
Often tell stories of how their friends who attend the public schools
Say that "the work in the public schools is harder"
Just recently two of the children I am teaching
Came to me and said
"Teacher, so and so said that they do harder work than we do"
I said to them
"What do you mean 'harder work'?"
I showed them our math
"Let me tell you something" I said
"The reason why so-and-so says they are doing harder work in the public schools
    is probably because she doesn't understand it
She's in a classroom with 30 kids
You are in a classroom of 4 children
You two understand the work we are doing like the back of your hands
You two know how to do expanded form, standard form
Maybe the other girl doesn't understand how to do these things
So, I think that's what is happening
It's not that you're doing easier or harder work than her
The difference is that you understand the work you're doing and maybe she
    doesn't"

When the children I teach tell me these stories
I know these are the stories they are hearing about our Band school
I know the story of our school
The perception out there (Motioning with her hands to show the bigger
    community)
Is that while we may be teaching the curriculum it's watered down
(Word image from Lucy's experiences storied in narrative inquiry circles on September 24,
2006; October 10, 2006; & November 7, 2006)

As Lucy storied these earlier noted experiences in narrative inquiry circles
over the fall months of 2006, she wove together her then present experiences
as a graduate student, as a teacher, as a mother, and as a member of the
community of Membertou with her past experiences as a child in a public

school context in which the values, the stories her non-*Mi'kmaq* teacher lived by, shaped her experiences in school. In this temporal movement across time and place Lucy made visible her rubbing up against the intergenerational narrative reverberations of colonization shaping public educational contexts. However, in seeking to be included in and to balance the complexities of becoming a teacher in the midst of these intergenerational narrative reverberations, we saw that the stories Lucy lives by hold much potential for threading numerous new possible intergenerational narrative reverberations.

As we traced the complexities Lucy experienced as she navigated a post-secondary place where she lived as a graduate student, the place of Membertou School where she lived as a teacher, and the public school system where she lived as a mother, we saw multiple ways in which she experienced a sense of disconnection through the imposition of values or stories not her own, stories which she felt she was expected to live by. Lucy began to unravel this thread in her becoming as she reflected upon experiences she lived in her graduate teacher education program. One disconnection Lucy noted in relation with this place was needing to attend summer courses which began on a national holiday, a day Lucy wanted to spend with her children and family. Instead, she found herself driving early in the morning to arrive in the class on time, only then to experience another sense of disconnection as she sat at the edge of the room, alongside additional students of *Mi'kmaq* ancestry, and was required to listen to the professors talking about themselves. Lucy named the tensions she experienced as shaped in multiple ways. Part of what she highlighted was that she felt unable to engage with the ideas and materials presented in the course because she could not express her knowing in ways that felt, to her, meaningful and respectful. Lucy also expressed a sense of feeling expected to participate in only one way which was within the group of *Mi'kmaq* students who were placed together to focus on language research. As someone whose life, including the learning of her ancestral languages, is deeply impacted as a result of the residential school experiences of her parents, which resulted in Lucy growing up without learning the *Mi'kmaq* language, she did not want to participate in the language focused group. This choice was as a result of not wanting, once again, to feel deficit.

As Lucy thought with these more present stories of experiences in her life she recalled similar experiences, similar feelings shaping her childhood experiences in a public school. As she storied these earlier experiences Lucy drew upon a poster of *Mi'kmaq* Treaty Day which is celebrated by *Mi'kmaq* communities every October 1st. Recalling the ways in which her "identity was pretty much taken away from ... [herself] in school," Lucy storied additional complexities she experienced as a child and youth in the public school system and, more presently, that her oldest son experienced in his journey in the public school system. Not unlike Lucy's more present experiences in the graduate course and as she watched her son experience the public school system, Lucy saw continuing intergenerational narrative reverberations shaping both her and her son's experiences. As a child in the public school system Lucy remembered that "all ... [she] ever knew about ... [herself] was that ... [her] ancestors were 'savages' and that ... she was an 'Indian' girl living on a *Mi'kmaq* reservation in Nova Scotia." Now as a mother, Lucy wondered why public schools continued to pay little, if any, respect to the lives of the *Mi'kmaq* children and youth in their schools. Lucy wondered, for example, why June 21st, National Aboriginal Day, a day of great celebration, importance, and significance for Aboriginal people across Canada is, for the most part, ignored. As she continued to think with these storied experiences of her son, Lucy returned to thoughts of herself as a *Mi'kmaq* teacher and her feelings that as a *Mi'kmaq* teacher in a public school her values, her stories to live by would be watched and that she would need to fit into the dominant institutional narrative.

As we continued to think in these multidimensional ways with Lucy's stories we saw that the intergenerational narrative reverberations of colonization which shaped Lucy's life as a child in a public school were continuing to shape her son's experiences in a public school as well as Lucy's experiences in a post-secondary place. Yet, as we simultaneously attended to ways we saw Lucy seeking to be actively involved in her becoming a teacher we saw that as a teacher alongside children at Membertou School Lucy is trying to support them to live and tell stories which interrupt the stories they are being told, stories in which their *Mi'kmaq* school is seen as less than and as not measuring up to what happens in the local public schools. In living out this new possible intergenerational narrative reverberation with the children Lucy celebrated their school, their community, and their knowing as each holding significant capacity. In knowing that she does not want to become "self absorbed" like she experienced some professors to be, what kept Lucy composing and living out these new possible intergenerational narrative reverberations was her strong sense of not wanting herself, her children or any child to continue to be harmed by intergenerational narrative reverberations which shape practices, policies, and values that harm someone's sense of self, their unfolding stories to live by.

Brenda Mary

Dear Journal
Back to education
I took my midterm tests even though the week before
I lost my oldest sister
And I was, and still am, going through this loss
It most likely will reflect on my work

I worked so hard studying for my language tests
Intro to *Ojibwe*
Structure of *Ojibwe*
Linguistics of *Algonquin* Language
Language Planning
Academic Writing
Curriculum Design and Methods
Traditional Seminars
Computers

For Intro to *Ojibwe* we had to remember and use home activities, furniture,
    geography, landscape, trees, rocks, animals, birds, fish, types and uses
Reading and writing roman orthography and syllabics for the structure
I am stuck on the terminology of VAI
The intransitive word
I do not know what it means and I know it's important
I am stuck there on the different structure terms and labeling
These are the places I'm lost on

Back to Curriculum Design and Methods
We need to come up with a vision statement of classroom management
What is my vision of classroom management?
I think we were kind of thrown off today because of the disagreement over the
    word "discipline"
I always forget to put the "c" after the "s" in discipline so I right click my mouse
    on the word that I spell wrong and it corrects the word for me
That is a skill in itself to be able to do that
That is a trick my sister showed me
In the same reoccurring thought I know I cannot be lazy to learn how to spell
    because when I am up in front of a class I will be expected as an
    educator to know how to spell in English

Which takes my thoughts to standardization of the *Ojibwe* language
Everyone wants their version to be the right way to spell a word
For example
The word "*miigwech*"
Is how I was taught to spell it by my instructor
I have seen others spell it phonetically
"*Meegwetch*"
They make it look so Englishized

I go with the way I was taught
"*Miigwech*"
And I see other words along the way spelled differently depending on the dialect
Minnesota *Ojibwe* is a different dialect from Manitoba *Ojibwe*
But we are all from the same language family

I like the word "language nests"
This must be something that the *Maori* speakers coined in New Zealand
I like that
"Language nests"
I need to learn more about it

I challenged myself to learn five words a day
Any kind of word
One that I do not know
How to spell it
Know what it means
The definition of it and to use it in a sentence
So here goes
My first word will be "language nest"
Next journal entry will have something so say about that
I heard that word used in a conference I attended in the last 12 months

As well as immersion or emersion
Is it an "e" or an "i"?
What is the difference in those words?
What do they mean?
I want to write about those two words and the word lexicon and morphology and
        the word intransitive verb
This is all so challenging
And vision statement of classroom management
And descriptive writing
Second person writing
All these things I need to know
So my head is full
And memory techniques, too
How do you memorize something?
How do you remember when you are put on the spot?
How much can you say about something?
Do you say a little or do you say a lot about a question?
Do you say anything at all?
Do you take a risk at being wrong?
Are you okay with being wrong?
Are you comfortable with making a mistake?

I did not even time my journal entry
I need to discipline myself to do that
Time management
So I need to stop now

It is 10:23
I am tired
Till next time
I know now what to think about and what to write about

Anniin Boozhoo
Niin, Brenda Mary
I want to journal today because it is *Maadinawe gizhigad*, Saturday
On to other thoughts

Dear Journal
1) *Aaniin enakamigak*?
2) *Aan enakamigak*?
What's happening?
What is the right way to say this? Would you say 1 or 2?
I have heard it said but I cannot remember what I heard

Anyway, it's registration time for me
I am eager to get this set up for the year ahead, 07/08
For my first year back I will be taking 24 credits in each of the next 3 years
Starting with education courses, teaching and learning K-8 six credits
Along with teaching and learning
Practicum
Also six credits in acting theory and practice, mime, improvisation
Into to science

This brings me to the part of how to ask questions
How do I ask questions confidently without looking stupid or feeling dumb?
When I ask myself these questions do I lack in confidence and courage?
This has taken me all day yesterday to look on the computer for the courses
This is what I found
There is one slot open that is going to fit for me for the EDUC requirement
Not sure if there is a spot for Theatre, for Acting Theory and Practice
No openings for Intro to Science
I can live with that but I may have to take an EDUC elective instead

I am on my way to come see you
I emailed [my education advisor] last week
She did not respond
I was asking her if I need to see her before I register
So I will come see you and see what you say
I think I need some kind of purple paper when I register indicating that I will be
    doing a practicum this fall, one day or half day this term or this fall
See you in a bit
I am dying for a smoke
Can we go have a smoke?
I will be there in a few minutes
Love from Brenda Mary

Learning how to be a teacher is exciting for me
I love learning what I am learning
For example, today we had a double period of Curriculum
We talked about definitions
After a student disagreed with the definition of discipline in the book we went
    into this big spiel about the meaning of discipline and policies, procedures,
    manuals in school divisions
We did individual searches on that word and brain stormed words that we will
    come back to so we will grasp how these words are used in that context
I found that very interesting even though I was going through personal matters at
    home
Being able to discipline myself on the spot how to handle my stresses
(Word image composed from Brenda Mary's journal entries written on July 27, 2007 &
October 13, 2007 & two undated journal entries)

As Brenda Mary makes visible in her storied experiences, she experienced multiple life complexities both in and outside of the post-secondary place she attended. The earlier word image, composed from Brenda Mary's journal entries, began with Brenda Mary telling of her experiences of losing her oldest sister. Yet, in the midst of this experience, Brenda Mary's life as a teacher education student carried on: she still wrote the midterm exams and continued to attend classes while she simultaneously tried to find a place in the midst of a very full term to make sense of her loss, and to grieve. Not finding this time or place left Brenda Mary concerned that she may not do well on her midterm exams. As she highlighted, the many courses in which Brenda Mary was registered seemed to swirl about her as she tried to "handle ... [her] stresses."

Participating in the courses also created additional complexities. From her list of subjects Brenda Mary shows that many of her courses were language focused. While Brenda Mary was excited to study *Ojibwa* she struggled with how to learn the dialects in ways that are honouring of their origins. For example, Brenda Mary knew that attempting to learn any of the dialects by simply placing English phonetic rules onto the words is not helpful. While she struggled as she saw that there is a movement to standardize the spelling of words from the differing *Ojibwa* dialects, Brenda Mary was uncertain about how otherwise to proceed. What seemed to keep Brenda Mary trying to learn the differing dialects in ways that felt respectful were her memories of hearing the differing dialects spoken earlier. As she called forward these memories Brenda Mary sensed that in order to learn each dialect she needed to hear them spoken. These connections between place and dialect differences were important for Brenda Mary to remember as doing so gradually supported her to begin to compose a counterstory to live by. Even though doing so did not seem to immediately ease the complexity Brenda Mary was in the midst of experiencing, in her living Brenda Mary was threading a new possible intergenerational narrative reverberation, a reverberation that resisted the need to standardize the many beautiful and differing dialects of the *Ojibwa* language.

Another complexity Brenda Mary negotiated was her need to represent her knowing through the use of a computer. Although she continued to try to learn how to use a computer she found this difficult. In storying her tensions with these experiences Brenda Mary made visible the multiple layers shaping this complexity. Not only was the dominant use of the computer difficult because Brenda Mary needed to learn how to operate particular computer programs, but it was also difficult because she needed to switch from embodied and oral ways of knowing to representing her knowing in a typed or written representation. While English is Brenda Mary's first language she is far more comfortable with spoken English.

In addition, as she lived in the midst of multiple courses in one term Brenda Mary needed to also be thinking about and getting registered for a second term. This, again, because of the dominance of the computer in this process, created many complexities. The process of registering for the next term's classes increasingly filled Brenda Mary with feelings of being overwhelmed. For example, as Brenda Mary tried to register in the particular courses that worked in her time table, the further she moved into making her time table, the more complexity she experienced as she increasingly had fewer time options to choose from for the differing requirements of her program. Brenda Mary reached out for help, initially by attempting to meet with her academic advisor and when this did not work, she contacted Mary who was, at that time, a Director of an Aboriginal Student Services Centre.

As we continued to think with these storied experiences in Brenda Mary's life we wondered what might have happened had Brenda Mary not known Mary. This wonder continued to live with us as we, over time, learned of cutbacks to supports for Aboriginal post-secondary students. While funding for post-secondary has always been limited and tenuous for Aboriginal post-secondary students, what Brenda Mary showed us as also significant were the need for supports, cultural, emotional, and spiritual supports. Across Brenda Mary's journal entries she made evident her interest in learning and her passions for becoming a teacher. For example, while Brenda Mary had not yet had opportunities to learn more about the language nests in New Zealand she was certainly interested in doing so. What seemed to sustain the stories Brenda Mary lived by as she negotiated the complexities she experienced in her journey of becoming a teacher were the ways she continuously puzzled through these complexities, attempting to feel included as she thought through each complexity by thinking with stories of experiences she had lived outside of the post-secondary place. In this way, Brenda Mary reconnected with her home, with learning she experienced there and in her community. In doing so she simultaneously threaded other new possible intergenerational narrative reverberations, reverberations of hanging onto her storied experiences lived in places and relationships outside of post-secondary places.

Khea

When I first applied to become a teacher
I was streamed into the elementary teacher education program but I wanted
    secondary
There was a lot of competition for *Mi'kmaq* teachers to get into education
The university only had two allocated seats for Aboriginal students
One seat in elementary education, one seat in secondary education

Although the university that accepted me into elementary was my first choice I
    attended another university much farther away from my home because I
    really wanted to be a secondary teacher
The university I attended has an affirmative action policy in place but while I was
    a student there
And in the many years since
I've learned that lots of people in this province believe that the university I attended
    has low standards because they accept so many students of *Mi'kmaq* and
    of African Nova Scotian backgrounds
The programs
Like education, social work, and law
These programs have the largest numbers of students of *Mi'kmaq* and of African
    Nova Scotian backgrounds
Are labeled as having lower standards

It's very difficult
Even though I got into that university
I did struggle
Because there were so few people who were not of the mainstream

When I first started law school
There was this very talented Aboriginal woman on the faculty
But she left because she grew tired of fighting the racism of her colleagues
And the university administration
The last straw
Happened one day when this upper middle class male student
Told her she was nothing

But a "stupid squaw"
Because he didn't like the mark she gave him on a paper
(Word image composed from Khea's experiences storied in a narrative inquiry circle on
January 28, 2006)

As made visible in the experiences Khea storied earlier, from the beginning of her journey to become a teacher, she has attempted to have voice in the decisions affecting her. We saw this first when, although she was accepted into the university which she wanted to attend, and which was closer to her home, she made a hard choice to stay true to her dream of becoming a secondary teacher. At that time, there were only limited spaces available for *Mi'kmaq* students to enter into the secondary teacher education program. This situation shaped competition for those few spaces within Khea's and within other *Mi'kmaq* communities in the province. It also shaped the need for making some hard decisions. For example, Khea's choice to not enter into the elementary teacher education program meant that she needed to leave her community and attend a university at a substantial distance from her home and family.

As she studied at this distant university, Khea gradually realized that even though this post-secondary place was shaped by an institutional narrative of affirmative action, how this institutional narrative was lived out was quite different from what was intended. For example, not long after Khea entered into the teacher education program she learned of the story circulating, not only on campus but around the province, that because she and other students who were of *Mi'kmaq* or of African Nova Scotian ancestry were actively recruited into education, law, and social work programs, this post-secondary place was perceived as having "lower standards." As well, even though the university had adopted an affirmative action policy, Khea storied the struggles she experienced because there were few students not of the "mainstream." In this way Khea made visible that the dominant ways of being in this post-secondary place still felt shaped by dominant narratives more supportive of, resonant with, and comfortable for students of the "mainstream."

In Khea's continuing reflection on these storied experiences she high-lighted that because of the dominance of more mainstream narratives, the lives of faculty not of the mainstream were also impacted. As we continued to think with Khea's storied experiences over time, Khea often talked more about this experience, highlighting that the "upper middle class male student" who called the Aboriginal faculty member a "stupid squaw" seemed to face no consequences for living out this racist story. Although Khea did not tell stories of composing counterstories to live by as she storied her navigating these experiences in this post-secondary place, in her living we see that she was doing so. Khea had a dream of becoming a secondary teacher and this was the post-secondary place which made a space where she could realize her dream. But, to sustain herself in this place, Khea needed to compose a counterstory to live by of not leaving. In sustaining this story to live by both in her living in this post-secondary place and today as she continues to hear stories on the broader social landscape that this post-secondary place has lower standards, we see the new possible intergenerational narrative reverberations which Khea's counterstory to live by holds potential for shaping, reverberations of not leaving and of honouring difference, instead, of sameness in relation with standards.

Jennifer

I was working with a classmate
She was inquiring about my views on the historical happenings between
    Native Peoples and Europeans and the present day impacts and situation
We spoke at length on this topic
Questioning one another and sharing musings
As the topic was explored
This classmate established that she was not of Aboriginal ancestry
But was interested to know of my opinion
She was also seeking clarification on the historical events that occurred
And the accuracy with which they are recorded
As well as their significance

I shared what I could of my own understanding
I told her that I was not an authority on the subject and was not trying to be
Our project required that we seek out resources in order to present a historical
    picture of the interactions between Native Peoples of Canada and
    European settlers
This classmate challenged herself to write up a history that could be presented to a
    grade 6 class
The result was not what I expected
I was surprised and confused at what she presented
Such phrases as:
"The missionaries built hospitals so that they could care for aboriginals when they
    were sick"
And
"They (Europeans) showed them (Aboriginal people) how to farm so they
    wouldn't always have to hunt for food"
This was accompanied by cartoonish "clipart" portraying a young Aboriginal
    male and female dressed in "traditional" skins with a feather head band

I believe that any educator
Aboriginal or not

Should see the errors in this particular presentation
I did not get a chance to give her my opinion of the write up
But another classmate told her of my surprise
Her response was to call me a "reverse racist"
She also said, "What does Jen expect? I'm white!"

I have no other way to explain her behaviour
Except to say
She has a narrow perspective on this issue
Is being defensive because I did not discuss this with her directly
Which I wish I had done
And is now retaliating against me because she "lost face" in the process

What I expect from her
Is what I would expect from any educator
Impartiality and professionalism
I expect her to take a good look at the situation and respond intelligently
Not to throw some oxymoronic term at me
I expect the same from myself as well
To try to resolve this conflict, not avoid it
I tried to contact this person to go out for coffee
I've made two attempts (left messages)
She never got back to me
(Word image composed from Jennifer's experiences storied in a journal entry written in March 2006)

In this journal entry Jennifer highlights an aspect of post-secondary education which has been highlighted both in this chapter and elsewhere: the tensions which arise between Aboriginal and non-Aboriginal students as they seek to make meaning of Canada's complex history. Jennifer stories her interest and commitment to engaging in this kind of complex conversation with her classmate and stories her classmate as equally committed. However, somewhere in the process or maybe in the passage of time, Jennifer's classmate develops a resource in which Aboriginal people are only portrayed in ways already well known from the well worn colonial narrative of Canada's past. In this dominant colonial narrative the Europeans are always constructed as saviors of the "primitive" Aboriginals; there is most often no mention of the ways in which Aboriginal people supported the Europeans or of the ways in which the Europeans gradually stole the land, resourcefulness, and identities of Aboriginal people.

At the time when Jennifer's classmate shared the Grade 6 resource she had made, Jennifer did not respond as there was no time in class to do so. However, she did respond outside of class time and in this way her concern about her classmate's understandings traveled back to the classmate. In the second-hand response which Jennifer learned of from other classmates she heard that her classmate now saw her as being racist. This response concerned Jennifer and she tried to reconnect and to have a conversation with her classmate. Her classmate never replied and as a result this important conversation has yet to happen.

What stood out for us as we co-inquired into Jennifer's story of this lived experience is the vital need for students of Aboriginal and non-Aboriginal ancestry to have spaces in their post-secondary places where having complex conversations can unfold. We imagine that in these kinds of spaces and conversations in post-secondary places many new possible intergenerational narrative reverberations might take shape and begin to unfold.

Lulu

When students know teachers care about them
They will stick with school even when things are hard
I carry this knowing as a teacher because I learned it when I was in the B. Ed.
        program

We had a fire in our house
The fire happened in late December
I did not return to the university when the January term began
The second week I was away the Chair of the Education Department called me
We were staying in a hotel
All of us
My husband, our four children, and me
We were squeezed into one small hotel room
It was overwhelming
I did not feel it was right
For me
To leave my family and go back to school
This would have meant we were apart from Sunday evening until Thursday evening
Every week

When the Chair called she asked how we were doing
Then, she said she wanted me to know she had heard about our house fire and that
        she and the faculty were thinking about us
She asked if there was anything she could do to support us
She also told me she hoped I would come back and finish the program
I was only 11 weeks away from graduating with my B. Ed.

The next week, she called again
This time, she said
That if I came back that week and caught up on all of my assignments by Thursday
I could still finish the program
My husband, children, and I talked about my going back to finish and we decided

that I should go
It was important to all of us that I finish the B. Ed. program

So, we went to the laundry mat in town
Got all of the laundry caught up
Then I headed to the town where the university was located

Lucy was one of my roommates that year and so was Marsha (pseudonym)
They both helped me so much
We were working until 3 a.m. on my assignments and then going to classes during
    the day
But we made it
I could not have made it without Lucy's and Marsha's and my family's support

Because this Chair called and supported me like she did
I knew I could make it
On Thursday when I handed in all of my assignments
She told me she knew I could do it

When I graduated that spring
I stopped by her office to thank her and she told me that my stopping to say thank
    you meant more to her than a bouquets of roses

Now, I'm in a graduate program
In this one summer course I felt like I was seen as not as dedicated to teaching
I felt this way because the students who only drove
A short distance
They were always at the class early
Nobody in that room seemed to know that every summer
As part of who we are as *Mi'kmaq*
We spend time on the island[4]
There is no running water and no electricity on the island
So every morning I had to get water from the lake to wash myself
Then, I had to walk across the island to catch a boat
At quarter to seven in the morning
Then, I had to hitch a ride to get to class in a town over 100 kilometers from the
    island

By the time I got to class I was always late
So I just sat on the sidelines because there were no other chairs left open
Every night I had to read all of the readings by candlelight
(Word image composed from Lulu's experiences storied in narrative inquiry circles on
September 8, 2007 & April 8, 2008)

As Lulu storied her and her family members' living through the damage
of their home in a house fire, she showed multiple complexities
simultaneously at work in her life. This house fire took place just as Lulu
was on the brink of going back to school, into the final semester of her

teacher education program. As Lulu and her family squeezed into the hotel room in the nearby city, she felt that returning to school was not an option; Lulu did not feel it was right for her to leave her family. In living by this story Lulu decided that what was most important was that the family needed to stay together to support one another.

It was the phone call from the Chair of the teacher education program that drew Lulu back into involvement in her studies. Not only once, but twice, the Chair called to encourage Lulu to return and to hear of ways she and the faculty could support Lulu and her family. These invitations to return and to have support were significant as Lulu and her family gradually decided that she needed to go back to school and to finish her degree. Her degree, as Lulu storied, "was important to all of us." In this way, not only was Lulu involved in the program, but so, too, was her entire family. When she returned to campus, two close friends, Lucy and Marsha, worked alongside Lulu to help her to catch up on missed assignments.

As we thought with these experiences in Lulu's life and ways in which the support of a Chair and a faculty, of family, and of friends supported Lulu to complete her B.Ed. degree, we talked about how rare and silent these stories of support often are in post-secondary places. Because post-secondary places are predominately shaped by dominant institutional narratives of one size fits all, Lulu's storying of and our thinking with these experiences made visible a new possible intergenerational narrative reverberation that pushes back against the reams of standardized policies and practices in universities. In this pushing back, lives, in all of their complexities and difference, become more central in decision making. This reverberation means that each life needs to be attended to as no one life is a model for the vast multiplicity of lives that enter into post-secondary places. At a time when financial cutbacks to post-secondary places are shaping larger and larger class sizes, this new possible intergenerational narrative reverberation of attending to lives, seems crucial.

As she later enrolled in a graduate program, Lulu's earlier storied experiences of invitation, consultation, involvement, and support dramatically shifted. Instead, she found herself sitting on the edges of the classroom. Not only was Lulu physically positioned at the margins of the classroom but as she interacted with peers in this space, she felt "like ... [she] was seen as not as dedicated to teaching." In this situation, and being or feeling positioned in these ways, no one came to know anything of the years of dedication that brought Lulu from her home community to the university to attend courses. Knowing Lulu's life, which we saw as hopeful in shaping new possible intergenerational narrative reverberations attentive to lives, might have positioned Lulu differently in the graduate course in which she was situated on the edges.

It's hard to imagine what the communities and our homes were like without us
  children
It must have been so lonely
Even today
Anyone who has family misses family when they are not together
I remember the times we would be preparing to leave for school
My Mom and Dad would go to bed without saying goodbye to us or even giving
  Us a hug
They could not face us leaving for school
Oh what pain they must have endured, too
All in the name of us getting civilized
I cry as I remember and write this
I wonder how many other households went through the same thing
We know what we want our First Nations students to learn
We all agree that respect is one of the foundations of what defines our values of
  our people
There are so many excellent teachings we can draw from
The hard work of collecting and doing the research based in the traditional
  teachings as the Elders have given us has really paid off
(Word image composed from Florence's journal entries written on May 1 & May 3, 2006)

For many years in my life after the Residential School I didn't think our language
  was important
So I did not speak it
In those years, too, I was teaching in a location far away from our people and
  language
But when I came home to visit, my father would say,
"Okay, you're home now, you speak the language now"
I would start to cry then because I wasn't fluent anymore and I'd say to him,
"Just give me a few days and I'll get it back"
But really I didn't think it was important because of the hardship it gave me
My language gave me hardship when I was at the Residential School and it gave
  me hardship when I came back home
I wouldn't speak at home and my father threatened to punish me
I think at that time I felt that my language had hurt me so much
But when my father died I just kept thinking
"I've got to keep my father alive. How do I keep my father alive?"
Then I realized that my father, and my mother, had given me a legacy
My language
That was 1974
That's when I became born again *Mi'kmaq*
I wanted to continue living everything my father valued
He was so proud to be *Mi'kmaq*
He was so proud of the *Mi'kmaq* language
He was so proud of the traditions
He was so proud of everything about who we are as *Mi'kmaq*

(Word image composed from Sister Dorothy's experiences storied in a narrative inquiry circle on January 28, 2006)

Who can deny that the intergenerational narrative reverberations of colonization have not shaped Brenda Mary's, Jennifer's, Jerri-Lynn's, Khea's, Lucy's, and Lulu's lives, past and present? In storying their lives they show this intergenerational shaping but, in their storying and restorying they also show additional aspects of their lives. In their living, today, Jennifer, Lucy, Jerri-Lynn, Lulu, Brenda Mary, and Khea are composing stories to live by that seek to counter, to interrupt the harm done to them and to their ancestors. Jennifer's, Lucy's, Jerri-Lynn's, Lulu's, Brenda Mary's, and Khea's counterstories to live by are filled with possibilities for shaping new possible intergenerational narrative reverberations. Will you walk alongside Jennifer, Lucy, Jerri-Lynn, Lulu, Brenda Mary, and Khea? Will you become part of the cultural, familial, linguistic, institutional, and social restorying to which they are reaching, toward which they are living?

NOTES

1. The Royal Proclamation of 1763 was issued by King George III. It recognized people of First Nations, *Metís, and Inuit* ancestry as distinct nations.

2. In his 2006 address at the Treaty Day Services in Halifax, Nova Scotia, Dan Christmas described how Article 6 of the Treaty of 1752 between the *Mi'kmaq* and the British includes that yearly, on the first day of October "the Mi'kmaq would receive presents and renew their friendship with the British" (*Mi'kmaq* History Month Proclamations from web).

3. Battiste (2010) describes the "established alliances with most of the Aboriginal nations before contact with Europeans. They were part of the ancient Wabanaki Confederacy made up of Maliseet, Penobescot, Passamaquoddy as well as relationships with the Mohawks at Caughnawaga and Oka of the Haudenosaunee Confederacy, and the Ottawa. The Mi'kmaq use the concept of Putu'swaqn or 'Convention Council' to describe the vast network of alliances" (pp. 5–6).

4. The island to which Lulu refers is connected with *Mi'kmaq* communities due to St. Anne's mission and the Grand Council of the *Mi'kmaq* Nation. Approximately 3,000 people gather on the island, just off the coast of the *Mi'kmaq* community of *Potlotek*, each July to celebrate the Feast of St. Anne.

CHAPTER 8

SHARING OUR FORWARD LOOKING STORIES

As you enter into this final chapter we ask you to imagine ...

Imagine all 10 of us gathered in a circle in a living room. Some women are seated on a couch; some are seated on a love seat, still other women are seated on chairs. It is a warm and sunny late-August morning; the patio doors are open, through which travels the sounds of birds and squirrels situated in nearby trees. Periodically, too, are heard the sounds of vehicles either on the main road at somewhat of a distance or more close by as they drive through the parking lot of Mary's condominium complex. Sunlight streams through the patio doors and a long, rectangular window at one side of the room; it dances on walls filled with the beautiful works of various Aboriginal artists. The wise eyes of two young children in a photograph gifted to Mary on a trip to Australia look out at us. We are also called into the earlier lives of Aboriginal people in Canada through *Nokomis'* paintings which she titled: Needing a Rest; Broom Ball; Blue Berries in August; After School; Fading Day; and, Here We Are. The largest painting, of considerable size, which mesmerizes each of us as we look into the shining face of a teenage girl in a boat on a lake, creates many conflicting emotions. The young girl's face is poised upward as though she is experiencing sheer joy at being in that time and in that place; its title reads: "Oh, how I wish I were back on that road again." From Mary's stories we knew this is a painting of Helen Betty Osborne, a young Aboriginal woman from Norway House[1] who dreamed of becoming a teacher. However, part way through her journey Helen Betty Osborne was brutally murdered by four White men.[2] Reflecting on the spiritual connection she felt in creating artworks for a book portraying Helen Betty Osborne's life, Madison Blackstone (2008) writes that

> Helen Betty Osborne believed in her ability to achieve a dream of becoming a teacher. The obstacles she faced were great; the financial hardship, racism, leaving her

family. ... "The Life of Helen Betty Osborne" has truly been a spiritual experience for
me as an artist. She guided my hand and touched my life. Thank you Betty and to those
who allowed me the opportunity to, through my art, be loud enough for Betty. (p. 31)

In the moments after Mary shares these stories it was quiet in our circle of
women, quiet as we each lingered on thoughts of Helen Betty Osborne's life,
imagining what could have been otherwise.

Imagine that these inward imaginings gradually turn our attention toward
one another, and in particular, toward the lives of the six teachers in our
circle. Imagine that as we are each ready to begin, that Sister Dorothy's and
Florence's voices rise and fall as they each pray for this time together, our
final conversation as a whole circle of women. This was a time, a day, and an
August weekend of much: of much continued connecting and learning, of
much excitement, of much joy, of much sadness, and of much hope. We had
drawn out as long as possible the funding for our narrative inquiry. In just
over a month any remaining funding would need to be returned to SSHRC.
We knew that without additional funding it was very likely that we, our
circle of women, would never again travel from our differing life places
across Canada to gather together in the same room. Yet, while we were each
saddened by this reality we were, at the same time, filled with immense hope.
Yesterday we read and talked through the entire draft of our book. This was
an emotion-filled experience. For some of us yesterday was the first time we
read or heard one another's stories of experiences. Our stories alongside one
another's stories were, at times, overwhelming. However, in this meeting of
our storied lives we also felt intense hope for what our experience of our
lives might re-make, both within Canadian post-secondary education places
and within school, community, and family places.

Imagine that as Florence's and Sister Dorothy's prayers are finished we
begin to talk around our circle of women, gradually sharing our thoughts in
relation with two questions we collectively felt were important to reflect
upon as our narrative inquiry was coming to a close. These two questions
and our reflections in relation with them are now represented in the
upcoming sections of this chapter which, after the fact, were composed into
the form of a whole circle conversation.[3]

8.1. SIGNIFICANT ASPECTS OF OUR RELATIONAL NARRATIVE INQUIRY JOURNEY

Jennifer: There have been many meaningful experiences that have occurred
throughout our time together. Being a part of this work has not only allowed

me to develop a better understanding about myself and the path that I choose to take from this day on, but it has resulted in new friendships with women whose stories have become part of my own.

Brenda Mary: Meeting some other people in the same situations in a different part of the country, even one who attained an Order of Canada ... Sister Dorothy Moore, to have met her was very significant to me. And, the fact that we were able to travel to the eastern parts of Canada also is significant for me and hearing the other First Nation language of the people of Eskasoni and Membertou was music to my ears.

Jerri-Lynn: For me, some of the most significant aspects of our work together have included becoming more aware of who I am as an Aboriginal person. I learned so many life lessons from every single lady in our group. I learned from our Elder, Florence. I learned more about our *Mi'kmaq* friends.

Janice: Being able to connect from our differing locations across Canada, that's also been an important part of the strength that's happened. Maybe that will inspire someone who reads our book to keep trying to make connections across the country.

Lucy: I also find that stories make it more real. Like, you can't pretend that it didn't happen. These stories that we've told in the book, they are real, they really happened, and they are still happening. When a student in post-secondary reads these stories a light bulb might go on in their head. You know? Reality is going to hit them. It's not something they have only heard about in the media or, you know? It's actually written down now.

Khea: In our community, in our culture, stories are significant because they teach you things. There are teachings all the time in stories. Or, just for humour or for healing and it's all stories. In our culture stories are very valid.

Mary: Even though our narrative inquiry circles were so intense sometimes we still found humour and this helped us to continue sharing. Remember when Sister Dorothy brought those crazy glasses to our whole group narrative inquiry circle? We laughed the entire weekend!

Janice: When you come to know someone's stories, and as someone who has been able to know the stories that came forward, I have such a feeling of lives unfolding.

Sister Dorothy: When each individual person spoke, whether it was Khea, Lucy, or Lulu, that's relating to our group in Nova Scotia, they truly spoke from the heart. And, I could relate to so much of what they were sharing because of my own personal experiences but then, there were parts of it I really couldn't relate to because that wasn't my experience. However, I think the key was that we were sharing and we were sharing our gut feelings and we were sharing in an environment that was trusting.

Florence: After spending 5 years with a group of young women, it is difficult to narrow down some of the most significant aspects of our work together. As the

Elder I felt honoured to have been chosen and in the beginning was hesitant because of the intensity and the commitment required of the research project.

Lulu: When I think about how post-secondary was as a teacher, what stands out for me is to now be given a voice. From Kindergarten to today, I didn't know that anybody would care, but this research has given me a voice and it's going to be written.

Brenda Mary: I also thought about the fact that we get to express our thoughts and feelings about our experiences in the post-secondary setting and to be acknowledged in the form of written words through a book which will be published and used as a helping tool for others who enter through the same post-secondary doors as we did, the colleges and universities. This empowers us to be able to use the gift of education because we are told knowledge is power. From there the sky is the limit.

Mary: This is why I wrote *Pimatisiwin: Walking in a Good Way* and the article, *Is the Legacy of Residential Schools Relevant Today?* I wrote these for post-secondary students, for my family, and for institutions. I think they are helping to make change.

Florence: It was about the third meeting of the project that I knew the importance and presence of an Elder in the process. Even though Mary had told me that I didn't need to be there for every meeting, it became imperative that I was present at all meetings as Jennifer, Jerri-Lynn, and Brenda Mary started to share some of the challenges of being a student in institutions where they were attending. From thereon I made sure I was there at all the meetings. Mary and I, being veterans in Aboriginal education and our continued involvement in it for many years, gave us enough experiences to draw from to help the young women deal and cope with some of these familiar challenges that Aboriginal people often face.

Sister Dorothy: One thing that I hope can be an outcome from all of the times we have been together and forming this what is to be a book, it's my hope that whoever it is out there who picks up this book, and who might have preconceived ideas, attitudes, feelings about First Nation people, and those come from way back, and they come into the education system with that, all of what I have just said. But if that person picks up this book and is enlightened and is re-educated and would be maybe surprised and say, "Gosh, I never thought that First Nation people would have the difficulties that they have experienced because of who they are and I personally have contributed to it. Now I know, now I know, and now I want to change it; I want to move forward and be ever conscious of what I have learned in this book. That's my hope, that's my hope.

Jennifer: Another significant aspect of this work for me has been allowing myself to identify as Aboriginal. I went through a few phases in my life where I rejected my heritage. I felt ashamed and embarrassed to be Aboriginal on many, many occasions. I also felt many, many times that I was not "Aboriginal enough." When Mary first approached me to be part of this research, I worried that I had nothing to contribute because I grew up in a mostly non-Aboriginal community in the city, have mixed ancestry, and knew very little about my cultural heritage. I realize now that much of this is the reality for many Aboriginal peoples and can be directly linked to residential schools. It is good to finally feel okay to say that I am Aboriginal and to know that my stories might affirm the identity of other youth in a similar position as me.

Lucy: It's up to them, the future teachers, the future leaders, to make the changes. We are trying but it will be our grandchildren and our children who will have responsibility to keep things going, to keep going, to carry on the fight.

Khea: I think that's key right there, that they don't give up, that they continue to fight, that's the key. That's what I was thinking as you were talking. To not give up.

Lulu: Like residential school survivors, like we don't hear their stories, we don't hear their stories and I have a feeling that that's why they suffer. I don't know, but it's maybe way, way too painful for them.

Lucy: To be honest, my mom doesn't talk about it because it is too painful. It's too much.

Khea: But they're not healing.

Lulu: They're not healing.

Lucy: No, no, they're not.

Lulu: (Speaking in *Mi'kmaq*). If your mom shared maybe (speaking in *Mi'kmaq*) …

Lucy: But they do share amongst themselves.

Lulu: Yeah, but we don't hear them, we don't hear them, maybe even a little bit, nuh? We can help the people who read this book to become more aware of my teaching to today's children.

Lucy: It's the shame; it's the shame that was instilled in them. That shame is so deep.

Mary: I recognized that shame in my writing of my book and article and being at the University of Winnipeg for so many years and seeing adults in their 50s and knowing that they have been drinking, begging for money, not to give them an excuse, but knowing from my own experiences this is an impact of the residential school system. Lucy, I think that many survivors are like your mom, they find it too hard to talk about.

Jerri-Lynn: Being able to be in an environment where I could truthfully share who I was and learning not to let other people "burn my fire" out has also been significant for me. Through this I have realized that I do have something to contribute to the education system.

Khea: I think for me working on this book and having worked with Lucy, Lulu, Janice, Sister Dorothy, that for me it's been a time that I can't wait to spend with everyone, to hear everyone's stories, to celebrate one another, to hear and not just hear, but listen to everybody. It's been a healing journey for me as well to kind of also reconnect with people. Like me and Lulu reconnected. We are family but before this we never really talked. We had busy lives going different directions but this pulled us together. Lucy was a childhood friend whom I'd lost connection with and we got pulled back together again. Sister Dorothy, who I always have connections with but, again, having her here not for family things, to listen to her and to have her guiding our meetings, and to meet Janice. For me, that's what was so good about this work.

Janice: In the midst of our many, many times together and the stories shared I always felt that there is just an urgent need to hear the experiences you embody around language and culture. Often the people whose voices are listened to in education, at the government level, federal or provincial, sometimes they have an intellectual understanding of language and culture being important but I don't think that the practical, that the embodied knowing of what that actually means in a life, is understood or available on the broad Canadian landscape. There's a difference between knowing something of that experience in your head and being able to understand the experience in your heart. I recognize that I can never know in the same way that you each know this, each of you knows this in a way that I will never know it but I have grown much more away from a head understanding to a heart understanding or a whole body understanding of that significance.

Mary: When Jean and Janice and I first talked about this grant I knew this work would be intense but I also knew it would contribute. Again, this comes from my experiences working as a Native Student Advisor and believing that if we could develop a Centre where Aboriginal students would feel comfortable and safe. Even though some faculty and staff disagreed I knew in my heart I couldn't give up that dream.

Brenda Mary: As we spread our wings some of us will go back home to help improve situations there while others will stay in an urban setting. As for me, I want to go where people are hungry for the language. I want to take the language back home and help give it back through the very way it was taken through the education setting.

Jerri-Lynn: Coming together as a whole group, realizing that even across provinces we are still the same people, with similar experiences.

Jennifer: The area where this work had the biggest impact on me is when I realized that I had stopped "thinking." At one of our meetings, we were sharing stories about times when each of us had chosen to remain silent at critical moments, or times when decisions that affected us were made and we just went along with it. At that meeting, Florence quoted someone who said this to her once: "If you don't have an opinion, you're not thinking." I remember writing it down on my notepad—I still have that paper today. For some reason this statement had a big impact on me. It got me thinking and then it got me realizing that an opinion doesn't have much power unless it is voiced. Then I thought of all of those times that I was silent when important questions were being asked or when racist or ignorant comments were being spoken. I was then reminded about the role that I was working toward attaining and how important it was that I do as I would want my students to do. It is not always easy to speak one's mind or to challenge other peoples' thinking. It is something I believe is necessary though. This brings to mind another quote from an influential friend: "nothing worth doing is easy."

Florence: For me this was a significant aspect as the young women placed so much faith and trust in Mary and I. The young women found their voice and recognized they have the right to be heard. I know we all came out stronger and better individuals for being part of the research project. The outcome renewed and instilled pride to be who we are and what we will always be ... Aboriginal people.

Sister Dorothy: And I think that is a key because without that I don't think we, each of these women, who have shared what they've shared, and that's in the book, what they've shared is in the book. We've had tears, we've had laughter, we've had reflections from what was being shared. I also see the celebrations as well. I think we look so much forward to coming together because we felt, "I need to share this bit of something that I personally did that was successful" or "I can't wait to share this problem that I'm seeing that's happening to me in school" or "not only personally to me or to my children in the school because of who they are or what they are or what they've done" and sometimes those are negative and sometimes some of them are positive. I think my coming together with this group of women has always been a mixture of feelings. What can you take out of that but something very positive for one thing, very affirmative, very affirming for one another.

Jerri-Lynn: I remember presenting at the ANTEC[4] conference in Nova Scotia, and actually having people care about what we had to say.

Jennifer: This group has allowed me to accept myself as *Anishinabe*, when I believed I had nothing to offer the people. I spent many years of my life denying this part of me or minimizing my Aboriginal identity. This experience has given me strength, new friends, and a space to give voice to my experiences so that others might be validated and gain inspiration and strength.

Janice: I think that from the beginning we really wanted this work to be so different from what typically happens in research, which is often that the people who are working at universities they kind of just come and maybe ask some questions and they have people answer those questions for them and they learn a lot from that. But, we have been together for almost 6 years; it will be 6 years in October [2011]. So much in post-secondary is set up to be efficient, fast, and linear. Even if you think about funding, like when we received the funding, they really intended it to be for 3 years but then we asked a few times to have some extensions and, you know, I think that what we were trying to do is very different, very different—and when I say "what we were trying to do" it sounds like we, like any one of us had this grand idea of: "Oh, this is exactly what is going to happen" but, instead, we made it together along the way.

Brenda Mary: The growing pains and having the freedom to share and be heard, the sharing of tears, and the celebrating of triumphs. And learning about the technology of, for example, voice recorders and electronic mail and the technology of Skype making conferences through computer that was mentioned. I did not use that yet but, we most likely will at some point. But the fact that it is going to become a book is the most significant aspect for me and having my words in there: my words are maximum significant for me along with the other writers who are in or have already gone through post-secondary institutions. This does a lot for boosting my self confidence. It is significant to learn all about writing and leaving something behind for others to use in a good way because there is not too much recognition out there for First Nation people or writers. One writer I read said there is nothing there about us by us; it is all what Europeans wrote, European world view for Europeans. So to have something like this published eradicates that kind of talk and thought. There are First Nation writers writing about First Nation thoughts.

Jerri-Lynn: Creating bonds with wonderful women, that even though I may not see them regularly, we truly do have a special connection. Through this inquiry I have come to know that I am not alone in my experiences in school, family, life. Here, I have not been judged for what I thought or believe in.

Sister Dorothy: The women, each of the teachers, gained an enormous amount of strength. An enormous amount of believing that who they are and what they are doing is not only favourable but they are developing into true educators and it's out of this. The fact that three of the teachers gained their masters degrees is also a significant sign.

Jerri-Lynn: Mary and Jan have been strong leaders in this work. They are people who care about where we are going in life. They are role models.

Mary: Working alongside Jan we learned about one another along the way. I remember telling Jan it's okay to cry and to trust your heart and she's never stopped crying (laughter). I named her Two Rivers Woman because Sister Dorothy said that when Jan cries there's these two rivers down her face. I want to thank you, Jan, for walking with all of us in a good way.

Sister Dorothy: We believed in you, we trusted in you, we trusted you, we loved you and we loved the tears that came so often because these tears were real and you had reason to shed tears and we were all just there, right there.

Lulu: And, our book isn't just ... for teachers, it's for survivors, for abused women. I hope this book isn't just for teachers but also starving, surviving mothers, you know? I remember being a starving mother going to school.

Khea: And there's no colour or culture painted on that. That happens to women everywhere.

Brenda Mary: What might be significant, too, is to have add-ons for the book: Book 2, Book 3 but, that is yet to be seen, looking to the future.

Janice: I feel a deep gratitude to each one of you and to Sister Dorothy and to Mary and to everyone in Winnipeg. Wherever my life unfolds in the future I can just never imagine us not being connected. And, I want to say thank you. You have helped me to be a better mother because of your stories and who you are as mothers. I have had the privilege to be in your homes, to come to know your children, and your families and I think you are extraordinary mothers. When I think of your challenges and how hard it has been at times to be at university I am just humbled, incredibly. I think that because I have been able to hear and to learn from your stories I hope Ellee [my daughter] will be stronger in her life because of your presence in my life. There isn't a day that goes by for me at the University of Regina that you are not in me when I sit in meetings and I realize that we are enacting policy that would not work for you. That doesn't mean that I am not thinking about the many students who are of First Nations, *Métis*, and *Inuit* ancestry who actually come to the University of Regina—I am. But it's you who keep me wakeful because I know you. I don't know them yet. Knowing your stories now creates an inward knowing in me that makes me stop and question. I realize I have been given an incredible privilege to sit at this table with all of you all of these years and as a non-*Mi'kmaq* and a non-Aboriginal person this is HUGE, that gift. I want you to know that I will honour and respect this gift, forever. And, I know that I have many responsibilities.

Khea: And, it's a work in progress because I don't think it's finished; I think it is going to continue on. And, I think it's all continuous, it all meshes together because there's never a beginning and an end for us, it's ongoing and this book definitely reflects that.

Lucy: Yup. I just hope that whoever decides to read the stories reads with an open mind, first of all and to tell their stories, write them down, share them with other people. It's almost like a pay it forward thing because these stories, telling our stories, helped to heal us and then we just put our lives and our pasts in perspective and I think that's important. That's what I hope for the future.

Janice: Yes.

Lulu: Yup, for the future.

Lucy: Yes, that's what I want. That's what I hope.

Khea: It's all connected but, you need to know your past in order to know your future and that's what Sister Dorothy always says, and what Lulu says.

Lucy: Or you have to want to remember your past.

Khea: And, that's hard.

Lucy: Yes.

Khea: It's hard to move forward if you don't acknowledge your past.

Lucy: I think that's what this storytelling did for us.

8.2. CONTRIBUTING TO THE REMAKING OF POST-SECONDARY EDUCATION THROUGH RELATIONAL NARRATIVE INQUIRY

Janice: What about changing post-secondary because of this? How do you think this work will change those places or has it changed us so that we can do something different in post-secondary?

Lucy: I think THAT has occurred. I think, for me anyways, because when we got involved in this project we had to go back.

Khea: Um hum.

Lucy: I had to grow as a student and I had to really think about, "Why am I here?" and not to think it's because I want to do this book because at first that was my thought, "Okay I am only here because I want to be part of this research. I am not here for anything else." But then my thinking evolved and I was really there to better myself, as a woman, as a mother, and as a teacher and I wanted to make a difference within my family and within my school community. I just wanted to do something significant and I knew this was going to be huge in the end. I knew it was going to be huge and people are asking me about the book and I'm very modest, I don't really say anything until they ask. Usually someone is next to me and they say, "Oh, by the way, Lucy is part of this book project." That's what is happening. I think post-secondary made me better myself. In the beginning I didn't think we could actually change the dynamics of what post-secondary is but, being a part of this project helped me get through it and I am a better student because of this work.

Florence: As for the contributions this research project will make towards the reshaping of post-secondary education, ... has endless possibilities; it has promise and it has the potential to encourage other people in all facets of life to take time to listen to the stories of triumphs and challenges of the young people. Finding our voices in which to express ourselves freely without fear of reprise led us to excellent and lively dialogues that were so honest and sincere.

Jennifer: Through the sharing of our stories, I hope that post-secondary institutions can become places where people are encouraged to share their stories and experiences as a way for others to gain knowledge of the world outside of their own experience.

Brenda Mary: I see myself contributing to the re-making of Canadian post-secondary education by opening up myself to sharing in an open and honest way, from my level of entry, the grass roots level experiences. The first thing I experienced was cultural shock because nothing is the way it is at home: time wise, money wise, and learning wise. Learning how to discipline myself to do all the required readings so as to be prepared for class and to be alert in an 8:30 a.m. class to be prepared to participate while learning at the same time how to participate in a debate and to be prepared for it as you take on the opposing side and put yourself across as an intelligent person in your answer. This is in a political science class I am using for an example. Another example is being able to produce a 1500–2000 to a 5000 word essay while learning how to go through the processes of delivering the essay by the due date requires a person to manage their time wisely. Also, how to take notes that are going to be helpful at exam time and how to make your bibliography the way the professor wants it. These are all things I learned on the spot.

Lulu: I remember one professor. Remember my favourite professor! Just because I didn't talk in class I don't know if he thought I didn't understand or I just didn't want to talk or if I could talk or if I did talk, could I talk in *Mi'kmaq*? So anyways, I never spoke, I just sat there, sat there and he brought in a *Mi'kmaq* guest speaker, to talk about treaties or something. He was talking about *Mi'kmaq* culture and all that stuff. You know? And, the professor would ask me something; he would look over, he wanted me to talk. He wanted a reaction. I didn't talk. I wouldn't talk and after the class ended, I was just kind of slowing down, just waiting for everyone to leave. I guess the professor knew, too, because he was just kind of digging in his stuff and after class I went up to him and I said, "I'm not going to talk in class. I'm not going to ask or talk in class." I said, "I would if I could speak in *Mi'kmaq*." And, he said, "Well why didn't you?" "Cause I didn't know if the *Mi'kmaq* guy spoke in *Mi'kmaq* because he was speaking in English." It was like he was trying to find the words so I knew he didn't speak in *Mi'kmaq*. He said, "Lulu, you could have spoken in *Mi'kmaq*. Why didn't you?" But there was arrogance and then when I did my work and when I finished my work, I had to give details about this one, he said, "Lulu, you surprised me."

Khea: He said, "You surprised him?" See those are attitudes right there.

Florence: My hope is that people will read the book critically and be able to examine their own attitudes towards other people that are different from them. An incident happened at one of our last meetings that reinforces the need for these types of research projects to continue. In August, 2010 one of our research members became ill where it was necessary to phone for medical support. When the service people arrived at Mary's there were obvious assumptions made about us as people who happened to be all Aboriginal except for one of us. If Janice was not there I am not sure if our friend would have received any help at all! I have to mention this because these types of attitudes are what many Aboriginal people are faced with on a daily basis. I know there have been great strides made in education, and in other service areas for which I am grateful for. However, these efforts are undermined if there is no change in the attitudes of the people who provide these services and they are present in all facets of our lives.

Jennifer: It is so important for all individuals to consider the perspectives that differ from one's own. This practice or way of being in the post-secondary landscape will help to make it a place where all people can really belong, not just those who fit in to the dominant society.

Brenda Mary: Just coming through everyday obstacles, like getting enough rest and food and housing, with the budget we have to work with it is very difficult. As well as systemic and reverse racism. These are the everyday realities and areas that I need to be strengthened in as I continue to pursue my education degree. Learning how to manage the money I have to work best for me.

Janice: When I think about post-secondary and that we teach maybe for an hour and a half twice per week or even 3 hours once per week, I realize how little we often know the students who are there. And, school knowledge seems so much more important than cultural, familial, communal knowledge. I think a lot about how not to lose and how to make those openings in universities so that that knowledge is not lost but that it's valued. I think in education there is a multi-sided way in which we need to be engaging: one is for the person and who they can be and who they are becoming and also for how they will teach. If we in teacher education only teach students to care about the government documents, the mandated subject matter material, I don't think we are being responsible to them, and of course, also not to all of the children and the families and communities that their work impacts.

Sister Dorothy: It's a big thing. It certainly is because you have to listen to the mouth that feeds you, which is the government. If you value your job, your position, you're going to follow what's required by the government. The advantage to having community schools, First Nation community schools, is that you have all the opportunities to develop your students from way down in kindergarten to high school to be who they are. In the off-reserve schools you don't have that and that's where your fighting comes in because you cannot adjust the curriculum because it's so set and there's very little allowed in providing languages, culture, history, relating to other Nations or other minorities. There are blocks everywhere, everywhere, but there are far fewer blocks in the First Nations community.

Brenda Mary: I will put it this way, likening myself to the butterfly as it goes through its metamorphosis from its original state of a cocoon to becoming a beautiful butterfly. As it makes its way through, if we disturb the butterfly by trying to be helpful to it as it is building its strength, if we break the cocoon off the butterfly we would kill it, we would take away its life. It would not be strong enough to fly. If we try to help it we have to let it strengthen itself, not disturb it. This way it can pass through all its stages and finish to become a beautiful butterfly. As hard as it was for me I had to learn how to take myself through all the stages required in order to complete my degree. I still need to go through these stages of my metamorphosis to gain my educational degree, to be recognized as an educator.

Lulu: I hope that post-secondary educators ...

Janice: Like me ...

Lulu: Yeah, that when they read this book, they say, "Oh, okay, step back. Why are we teaching this way? I never knew. I never thought about that one or about this one. Why would they? It was White."

Lucy: Yeah, but that post-secondary professor has to be willing to pick up our book and read it, he or she has to be willing. I'll be honest, not every professor is going to want to buy the book and read it; they won't be interested in the topic.

Lulu: But my hopes would be that my professor who always wanted me to talk, I don't know if he wanted me to speak in English or what; he just wanted to hear me talk.

Khea: Or he wanted to hear your thoughts and now you have a book.

Lulu: The end result was that he was surprised. He took me aside and said, "Lulu, I was really surprised." I guess he wanted to hear me but I didn't want to talk and if I had this thought then it wouldn't come out the same in English so I kept it to myself, until I started writing. When I did my master's research project I was writing. *Atji* was driving me to St. FX and I was writing. You should see my writing! I'd say, "Pull over, pull over!" *Atji* would pull over and I would write and then it was like, "Okay, you can go."

Mary: You are reminding me of when I first started teaching in Education. I wanted to make a safe place where students could say their names and not be ashamed of who they are as both Aboriginal and non-Aboriginal students. What I learned from them and they also contributed because of what they said in the classroom.

What you have to say we might not understand it now but maybe in a month or a year we can say, "Bill or Karen said that."

Khea: I feel like I was like that too, Lulu, especially in high school. I didn't always have that confidence to say what was on my mind.

Lulu: But, (speaking in *Mi'kmaq*), maybe post-secondary would now say, "Oh my, here they are talking about that, we never thought about that." Maybe they would think now, you know, don't expect a White road? And it's not all professors. When I went to the first university, that was the best thing that ever happened that I failed, that I failed there. That was the best thing.

Khea: Why?

Lulu: Thinking back now, eehh? My sister got sick and one professor, he gave me an incomplete but I failed four and I said: "Oh, man." Anyways, that was the best thing that ever happened 'cause we had exams, in education we had exams. We never once, that whole year, went out to a classroom and then we had exams.

Khea: All theory.

Lulu: Yup, and I didn't learn anything. I didn't learn ANYTHING! But, anyways, that was the best thing that happened. But that was the whole setting up of the school: it was their way or the highway.

Janice: So, in part, what I think I hear you saying is that you see this book as supporting the next Aboriginal people and women or people who are reading this book in other places in Canada and around the world, even if they are of another nation.

Khea: Not just even Aboriginal people, just women, African women, just women at all, even women from old Gaelic communities in Ireland can definitely relate to a lot of these stories.

Sister Dorothy: We have to continue to try to make a difference and I think maybe this book will do some of that and will be a positive thing for some people. The most important thing is in the university education departments, this book can make such a difference. My experience of speaking with university students, not at St. FX,[5] it was elsewhere. Here were B. Ed. students, future educators who were sitting there, and I have used this expression, like a bunch of potatoes with eyes. You know? They were so indifferent and to talk about First Nation people was meaningless to them. I was invited to a class taught by a First Nation person and she had students sitting around and I was speaking and I could sense immediately who was not paying attention. I stopped my presentation and I just said to them, "You know I know some of you couldn't care less about what I am saying about First Nation education but, I guarantee that some of you who are in this circle will be applying to First Nation communities for teaching because you are all not going to be teaching in Nova Scotia. I guarantee that then you will be saying, "Why did I not listen?" I got their attention. We will always meet that in our education system. We will always meet it because it's that cemented prejudice against minorities but, particularly First Nation people in our population as a whole in Canada. And, the farther west you go the worse it is. Some of that is because of the poverty of First Nation people. A lot is because of the poverty. A lot of it is because people are living in isolated areas and they haven't had the opportunity to be who the Caucasians think they should be. And they never will be. That's how I see it. So us working in small communities, us working in our own areas, there's hope for us.

Janice: You always said a prayer when we started, Sister. Sometimes you might have brought a poem along as well for us to read and to think about. There was something in that process of doing that that got us ready, that changed us or opened us or that made us ready for the work we were going to do. I attend a lot of meetings in a day or in a week where I often don't say anything because I can't connect with the way in which we engage with each other in a meeting context. We use a process of communicating called Robert's Rules and through our work together I have increasingly decided that when a meeting is structured that way I am either not going to go or I'm not going to speak because I don't know how to communicate with other human beings in that kind of way. I guess what I'm trying to say is that what you have taught me about is the importance of starting and shaping a spiritual place in a conversation. I have a stronger sense of this today because of how you have lived with us. I don't think I have a lot figured out but I do know that you started us in a spiritual place and that shaped something different in how we lived with one another and our stories. Maybe when you would start us with a prayer, Sister, or a poem, maybe what happened was that all of who we are as people was drawn or could be there and maybe that was, maybe it was that openness to our wholeness, to emotion, to feeling.

Sister Dorothy: Yes, and a moment in time of reflection and collection to what will be. I think it kind of sets us in a different space from being out there and now we are in this space and I do think that's a spiritual part of it. Everybody in that space becomes one. It's no longer individuals and we are one and most of the time we are one because God has made us to be one. Whether we think of it in that way or not, it happens, in our spirits.

Mary: Sister Dorothy talks about spirituality and I remember that when the Centre was being built I was adamant that smudging would be allowed. The Centre is the only place in the university where smudging is allowed. Prior to that, I always got into trouble if we smudged. We got in trouble because I didn't ask permission from the building engineer. I said, "I'm not doing that!" But at the same time I already see things at the University of Winnipeg and other post-secondary places and I think from this book post-secondary places and also schools will think about providing safe places where students can learn and be who they are.

Brenda Mary: Now, today, I see myself contributing by sharing, using a part of the seven sacred teachings which is sharing in an honest way and not being afraid, being courageous to face what is in front of me, using what I learned skillfully, eloquently, and poignantly. It is like breaking free of old ways that did me no good.

Lulu: My voice is going to be heard, my words, my stories are there. Through this research, doing it, it's like the book, it's like, "That's me." We could never say, "That's me." But, when we finish the book it's like someone else could say, "Well, that's me. I've been through that. Well you go talk to her. You go talk to these women, how did they survive?" I was giving up, you know? Raising four children and going to school with four children, having children and going to school. Luh? Someone reading our book might think, "She did it so I have to talk with her." Or, they might think about our work, being teachers. I fought for the *Mi'kmaq* language classroom, to have one and now I have one and you know maybe someone else doesn't have one. So it starts from being a mother, to going to school, to finishing school, to being in a motel room, living in a motel room for 3 months and someone calls me and tells me, the Chair, she calls and says, "When are you coming back?" "Can I come back?" It's all these stories. The little things. You keep going, keep going. But, it wasn't all, you know you didn't get from here to here (motions to show a straight line) it's all like this (motions to show more of a back and forth movement) and a lot has changed. But it's from being given a voice, to being heard through the book or through the stories in the book.

Khea: That's good. I think it validates all your (speaking in *Mi'kmaq*), like how much of a hard, like how much it's been an ongoing battle. You have your little triumphs but I think when you are reading someone's stories about those they feel, like what Lulu said, "I can relate to that." Especially if you have somebody who is trying to make their place in the world and not feeling they belong here or they belong there. Like Jennifer's stories, like Jerri-Lynn. They're like, "Okay, there's people like me who still have that same acceptance problem." But look. I overcame it. I have become more accepted. Most of all I have accepted myself. You know, they've come to a place where they are comfortable with who they are and they celebrate themselves now and that is so important, especially for our women going through the education system. The education system was not designed for women in the outset, it was for men and if you are a Native woman on top of that so it's another whammy on top of that, other layers of struggles and things. You know? And, mothers, oh my!

Jerri-Lynn: Many people today still say, "Get over it" and "How can something that happened so long ago still affect you?" But it does. So much! If you don't have anyone showing you the way to love your child, how to be a good student, and go to school, to be a good housekeeper, etc., of course it can affect you. Life IS about choices, but if you don't have anyone in your life to give some sort of direction, then how do you know which way to go? I consider myself blessed. Even though my life was crazy growing up, I had some great people along the way to show me a better way to live. This is another way I believe that I can help contribute to post-secondary education. If I can be a light in just one student's life, by my story, then I think I have succeeded. University is hard. Never mind having a family on top of it. If other post-secondary students can see my and all the other ladies' struggles, and know that we have succeeded, and they in turn try harder to complete school, then I think that is also a success.

Janice: I really think that it's going to be important in the years to come with this book that YOU are each able to be contacted. Mary is the first author on our book and as long as she stays at a post-secondary place it's easy to Google her and find her, right? But I really believe that part of what we should be thinking about is having, maybe like, the Membertou Band Office, maybe the Eskasoni Band Office, for Brenda Mary maybe it's the Peguis Band Office, some way for readers to contact each of you. I think people are going to search for you when they read your stories.

Khea: Society has been designed it's been a man's world for centuries. And it's only, we as Native people have started to make our mark in the world just lately. This is not even just decades so it's a really new thing for Native women especially to be making their mark in the education field and getting their post-secondary education and stuff because it's, you know? We all know that this world has not been designed for women and if you're a Native woman on top of that. I mean it's typical for a Native person or any kind of physical minority and then if you're a woman on top of that. I mean there are places in our world that women still have no say in anything and are denied education.

Lulu: And in our being *Mi'kmaq*, it's not the case. Women rule, you know? (Speaking in *Mi'kmaq*) but, outside ...

Janice: In the dominant world ...

Lulu: It's hard ...

Khea: It's hard for that transition ...

Brenda Mary: We all have different strengths we need to build upon. I am working on being acknowledged for who I am in the post-secondary setting and the changes that need to happen for us in order to be a successful graduate.

Lulu: Even the language. Coming from home and then going to university and transitioning to the language and all up here (motions to her head) and the same with women's roles.

Janice: Yes, so in part, when you are in a course in post-secondary then how you get situated there as a woman and then as a *Mi'kmaq* woman and as a *Mi'kmaq* speaker.

Khea: Because no matter what course you are taking it's already noticed you're a woman and second thing or maybe even, I don't know what comes first that you are a Native, a *Mi'kmaq* person? And then, you are a woman? You know those are visible and right away you are going into a classroom where there are misperceptions about who you are and where you come from. You know it's there but it's not until later that it comes out, if it even comes out. I think it's better for it to come out than to go away on the sidelines as if it didn't happen. It's reality, right? And people's attitudes need changing and the only way you are going to change them is if you bring out the worst in them, their attitudes, and change them, their opinions. I mean all of the courses we've done we've changed a lot of peoples' opinions about who we are and where we come from.

Janice: One of the things I have learned by being able to be part of this with all of you is very linked with that. My parents would be classified as "uneducated" people because my dad had a Grade 8 education and my mom has a Grade 9 education and when I went to school I think they were seen as not important farming people. But something that I think all of our parents or families have tried to instill in us is to not lose who we are in the process of "being educated." You have all made me think so much more about how at the university we focus on a body of knowledge or a discipline of knowledge. I think in doing only that there's a real danger that we forget the living bodies of the people sitting right in front of us who carry all kinds of really significant, important knowledge. Because this is the dominant narrative it can create a lack of connection to students' personal, embodied knowing that they carry. And if in the post-secondary context, whether we say it in our words or treat students that way, like if we send that message that Lucy, for example, what you learned from being the daughter of a residential school survivor doesn't matter, then what are we doing in post-secondary?

Lucy: Yup.

Mary: I am remembering that male student in one of my courses who ranted and raved about having to take a course on Aboriginal education. He yelled at me, "Why are we learning about residential schools. It happened so long ago!"

Jerri-Lynn: I can see myself contributing to the re-making of Canadian post-secondary education because of the life experiences I have lived. I can give myself to the people I work with and the students I work with, especially Aboriginal teens, because in many cases, I have walked in their shoes, I know some of the difficulties, challenges, and triumphs that they are going though. I can do my best to make sure the real truth of our history is taught in schools. I can teach about forgiveness to those who have done wrong. I can be an example of growing up in difficult situations but, in the end becoming someone, of doing something with their life.

Lulu: I have a friend who is a teacher who is non-Aboriginal and when she's teaching *Mi'kmaw* Studies she calls my Uncle and he teaches her. He also often teaches her students.

Janice: What you are making me think about, in terms of post-secondary, I am the person who is valued in a post-secondary context because I have the Ph. D. and, yet, it is your Uncle who does all of this amazing teaching in the community.

Lulu: And same with me. Even with me, when I do something around Christmas time. I don't know about that. I never, I was never there, I didn't know what it was but, I asked this Elder, this nice woman Elder and she does it all. She does it all and then we take it outside the classroom and we do it and it's beautiful, nuh?

Khea: But you need to have those connectors, you need to have those people who link students with the educators outside the classroom.

Lulu: But, it was through stories, nuh? It was through stories that got my non-Aboriginal friend motivated, nuh? She heard it and then she felt it and now she is sharing it. It shows that you have to feel it. You have to go there, you have to feel it. It is one thing listening to it; it's totally different doing it.

Lucy: You have to wonder though, it makes me wonder though. If your friend was Aboriginal would they allow her to do that? Would they allow her to go outside her classroom and take students to a sweat in an Aboriginal community?
Khea: That's a good question.

Janice: That's a very good question and I think this is really, well the paper we wrote is really about all of the ways you get seen as not "real" teachers, right?

Sister Dorothy: If it's culture or language or history, whatever it might be. If there was a negative in one part, the role of the professor is to change the negative to something positive. And, I think, skipping a little bit back to our wonderful three women in Nova Scotia who you've worked with, I think what has come out is a strong conviction that who they are as *Mi'kmaq* women is truly the best thing in the world and their language, their culture, their history.

Brenda Mary: By doing this I have gained tools to add to my repertoire, thereby empowering myself and our First Nation and sounding our voices in the remaking of post-secondary education in Canada. We will have the last say from this day forward on how we need this post-secondary education to work for us First Nation people.

Janice: I think there are probably not a lot of books in Canada or other places where that sense of lives is so there, lives are so present in this book. That's something that I hope will change research and teaching and life at universities.

Jerri-Lynn: Though our collective voices, I believe we can show those who have chosen to ignore us, or those who have not met us half way in our schools, that we are also people of importance, that we have a voice, that we are diverse. Because of our histories, because of our experiences, we can help make post-secondary education better for those behind us.

Florence: Lastly, as the research project comes to end, the voices of these women will be heard as we move towards making stronger and better spaces where new relationships and partnerships will evolve for all of us to contribute for a better future for all.

These were our lingering thoughts as our narrative inquiry, and this book, came to a close, for now. We have lived in a narrative inquiry space for many years. By the time this book was published in 2012 our relationships, and our ongoing inquiry into our storied lives, will have shaped almost 7 years of our lives. We say "Welalio" ... "Miigwetch" ... "Thank You" to one another and we say "Welalio" ... "Miigwetch" ... "Thank You" to you, a reader of this book. There is much that needs changing in post-secondary education in Canada and elsewhere. Our narrative inquiry has shown us that, together, as warrior women, as warrior people, in relation with one another and through narrative inquiry, we can re-make post-secondary education and we can keep co-composing and living by new possible intergenerational narrative reverberations. It is in our composing and living of these new possible intergenerational narrative reverberations that we will become heard, that change will happen.

NOTES

1. Norway House is located in northern Manitoba, Canada.
2. The Aboriginal Justice Inquiry's Conclusion into the death of Helen Betty Osborne highlighted that "It is clear that Betty Osborne would not have been killed if she had not been Aboriginal. The four men who took her to her death from the streets of The Pas that night had gone looking for an Aboriginal girl with whom to "party." They found Betty Osborne. When she refused to party she was driven out of town and murdered. Those who abducted her showed a total lack of regard for her person or her rights as an individual. Those who stood by while the physical assault took place, while sexual advances were made and while she was beaten to death showed their own racism, sexism and indifference" (Robertson & Blackstone, 2008, p. 30).
3. Our plan for our last whole circle of women gathered in Winnipeg for a weekend in late August 2010 was to spend the Sunday in conversation around two questions which we felt were important to reflect upon as our narrative inquiry was coming to a close. These two questions were: (1) What, for you, have been the most significant aspects of our work together?; and (2) How do we each see ourselves contributing to the re-making of Canadian post-secondary education? Coming together in conversation was a central aspect of our unfolding narrative inquiry.

However, our plans for that Sunday quickly changed when one woman in our circle suffered a stroke and was hospitalized. In the months afterward some of us wrote reflections in response to these two questions while others of us engaged in tape recorded conversations. As a result, while we were no longer able to actually live out a final whole circle conversation, we drew upon these field texts to compose this chapter in the form of a conversation.

4. ANTEC represents the Atlantic Native Teacher Education Conference which is held every second year in differing Aboriginal communities in Atlantic Canada.

5. St. FX refers to St. Francis Xavier University in Antigonish, Nova Scotia, Canada.

REFERENCES

Andrews, M. (2007). Exploring cross-cultural boundaries. In D. J. Clandinin (Ed.), *Handbook of narrative inquiry: Mapping a methodology* (pp. 498–511). Thousand Oaks, CA: Sage.

Archibald, J. (2001). Sharing aboriginal knowledge and aboriginal ways of knowing. *Canadian Journal of Education, 25*(1), 1–5.

Archibald, J. (2008). *Indigenous storywork: Educating the heart, mind, body, and spirit.* Vancouver, BC: UBC Press.

Archibald, J., & Urion, C. (Eds.). (1995). Honoring what they say: Postsecondary experiences of First Nations graduates. *Canadian Journal of Native Education, 21*(1), 11–221.

Augustine, M. (2002). *Educational Needs Assessment Atlantic Region, For the Seven Generations Post-Secondary Education Conference,* Atlantic Policy Congress (APC) & Indian and Northern Affairs Canada, Atlantic Regional Office, Amherst, NS.

Basso, K. (1996). *Wisdom sits in places: Landscape and language among the Western Apache.* Albuquerque, NM: University of New Mexico Press.

Bateson, M. C. (1989). *Composing a life.* New York, NY: HarperCollins.

Bateson, M. C. (1994). *Peripheral visions: Learning along the way.* New York, NY: Harper.

Bateson, M. C. (2000). Full circles, *overlapping lives: Culture and generation in* transition. New York, NY: Ballantine.

Battiste, J. Youngmedicine. (2010). *Honouring 400 years – Kepmite'tmnej.* Sydney, NS: Mi'kmaq Grand Council.

Battiste, M. (2004, June). Animating sites of postcolonial education: Indigenous knowledge and the humanities. Paper presented at the Canadian Society for the Study of Education, Winnipeg, MB.

Battiste, M., & Henderson, J. (2000). The importance of language for Indigenous knowledge. In M. Battiste & J. Henderson (Eds.), *Protecting Indigenous knowledge and heritage: A global challenge* (pp. 73–85). Saskatoon, SK: Purich Publishing.

Benham, M. (2007). Mo'ōlelo: On culturally relevant story making from an Indigenous perspective. In D. J. Clandinin (Ed.), *Handbook of narrative inquiry: Mapping a methodology* (pp. 512–533). Thousand Oaks, CA: Sage.

Bouchard, D. (1994). *The meaning of respect.* Winnipeg, MB: Pemmican Publications, Inc.

Bouchard, D., Martin, J., Cameron, K., & Swampfox. (2009). *Seven sacred teachings: Niizhwaaswi gagiikwewin.* Vancouver, BC: More Than Words Publishers.

Butler-Kisber, L. (2002). Artful portrayals in qualitative research. *Alberta Journal of Educational Research, 48*(3), 229–239.

Cajete, G. (2001, February). Finding face, finding heart and finding foundation: The making of an Indigenous teacher. Paper presented at The Banff Centre Aboriginal Leadership Symposium, Banff, AB.

Canadian Council on Learning. (2009). *Post-secondary education in Canada: Meeting our needs? (Executive summary).* Ottawa, ON: Author.

175

Canadian Institutes for Health Research. (2005 – Draft Document). *CIHR guidelines for health research involving Aboriginal Peoples*. Ottawa, ON: CIHR Ethics Office.

Canadian Race Relations, X. (2003). *Learning about walking in beauty: Placing Aboriginal perspectives in Canadian classrooms*. Ottawa, ON: Author.

Carr, D. (1986). *Time, narrative and history*. Bloomington, IN: Indiana University Press.

Castellano, M. B., Davis, L., & Lahache, L. (2000). *Aboriginal education: Fulfilling the promise*. Vancouver, BC: UBC Press.

Chung, S. (2008). *A narrative inquiry into the interwoven intergenerational stories of immigrant children and mothers*. Unpublished master's thesis, University of Alberta, Edmonton, AB.

Chung, S., & Clandinin, D. J. (2009). The interwoven stories of teachers, families, and children in curriculum making. In M. Miller Marsh & T. Turner-Vorbeck (Eds.), *(Mis)Understanding families: Learning from real families in our schools*. New York, NY: Teachers College Press.

Clandinin, D. J., & Connelly, F. M. (1992). Teacher as curriculum maker. In P. W. Jackson (Ed.), *Handbook of research on curriculum* (pp. 363–401). New York, NY: Macmillan.

Clandinin, D. J., & Connelly, F. M. (1994). Personal experience methods. In N. Denzin & Y. Lincoln (Eds.), *Collecting and interpreting qualitative materials* (pp. 413–427). London: Sage.

Clandinin, D. J., & Connelly, F. M. (1998). Asking questions about telling stories. In C. Kridel (Ed.), *Writing educational biography: Explorations in qualitative research* (pp. 202–209). New York, NY: Garland Publishing, Inc..

Clandinin, D. J., & Connelly, F. M. (2000). *Narrative inquiry: Experience and story in educational research*. San Francisco, CA: Jossey-Bass.

Clandinin, D. J., & Huber, J. (2002). Narrative inquiry: Toward understanding life's artistry. *Curriculum Inquiry, 32*(2), 161–169.

Clandinin, D. J., Huber, J., Huber, M., Murphy, S., Murray Orr, A., Pearce, M., & Steeves, P. (2006). *Composing diverse identities: Narrative inquiries into the interwoven lives of children and teachers*. New York, NY: Routledge.

Clandinin, D. J., Murphy, M. S., Huber, J., & Murray Orr, A. (2010). Negotiating narrative inquiries: Living in a tension-filled midst. *Journal of Educational Research, 103*(2), 81–90.

Clandinin, D. J., Murphy, M. S., & Huber, J. (2011). Familial curriculum making: Re-shaping the curriculum making of teacher education. *International Journal of Early Childhood Education, 17*(1), 9–31.

Connelly, F. M., & Clandinin, D. J. (1988). *Teachers as curriculum planners: Narratives of experience*. New York, NY: Teachers College Press.

Connelly, F. M., & Clandinin, D. J. (1999). *Shaping a professional identity: Stories of educational practice*. New York, NY: Teachers College Press.

Connelly, F. M., & Clandinin, D. J. (2006). Narrative inquiry. In J. Green, G. Camilli & P. Elmore (Eds.), *Handbook of complementary methods in education research* (pp. 375–385). Mahwah, NJ: Lawrence Erlbaum.

Council of Ministers of Education. (2008). *Backgrounder on the CMEC Aboriginal education action plan*. Ottawa, ON: Author.

Craig, C., & Huber, J. (2007). Relational reverberations: Shaping and reshaping narrative inquiries in the midst of storied lives and contexts. In D. J. Clandinin (Ed.), *Handbook of narrative inquiry: Mapping a methodological landscape* (pp. 251–279). New York, NY: Sage.

Dewey, J. (1938). *Experience and education.* New York, NY: Collier MacMillan Publishers.

Ermine, W., Sinclair, R., & Jeffery, B. (2004). *The ethics of research involving Indigenous peoples.* Saskatoon, SK: Indigenous Peoples' Health Research Centre.

Fitznor, L. (2002). *Aboriginal educator's stories: Rekindling Aboriginal worldviews.* Unpublished doctoral dissertation, Ontario Institute for Studies in Education of the University of Toronto, Toronto, ON.

Grant, A. (2004). *Finding my talk: How fourteen Native Canadian women reclaimed their lives after residential school.* Calgary, AB: Fifth House Books.

Greene, M. (1995). *Releasing the imagination: Essays on education, the arts, and social change.* San Francisco, CA: Jossey-Bass.

Hampton, E. (1995). Toward a redefinition of American Indian/Alaska Native education. In M. Battiste & J. Barman (Eds.), *First nations education in Canada: The circle unfolds* (pp. 5–46). Vancouver, BC: University of British Columbia Press.

Hong, Y. S. (2009). *A narrative inquiry into three Korean teachers' experiences of teaching returnee children.* Unpublished doctoral dissertation, University of Alberta, Edmonton, AB.

Huber, J., & Clandinin, D. J. (2002). Ethical dilemmas in relational narrative inquiry with children. *Qualitative Inquiry, 8*(6), 785–803.

Huber, J., & Clandinin, D. J. (2005). Living in tension: Negotiating a curriculum of lives on the professional knowledge landscape. In J. Brophy & S. Pinnegar (Eds.), *Learning from research on teaching: Perspective, methodology, and representation* (Vol. 11, pp. 313–336). Advances in Research on Teaching. Kidlington, Oxford, UK: Elsevier Ltd.

Huber, J., Graham, D., Murray Orr, A., & Reid, N. (2009). Literature conversations for inquiring into the influence of family stories on teacher identities. In M. Miller Marsh & T. Turner-Vorbeck (Eds.), *(Mis)understanding families: Learning from real families in our schools.* New York, NY: Teachers College Press.

Huber, J., Keats Whelan, K., & Clandinin, D. J. (2003a). Children's narrative identity making: Becoming intentional about negotiating classroom spaces. *Journal of Curriculum Studies, 35*(3), 303–318.

Huber, J., Murphy, S., & Clandinin, D. J. (2003b, invited). Creating communities of cultural imagination: Negotiating a curriculum of diversity. *Curriculum Inquiry, 33*(4), 343–362.

Huber, J., Murphy, M. S., & Clandinin, D. J. (2011). *Places of curriculum making: Narrative inquiries into children's lives in motion.* London: Emerald.

Huber, J., & Whelan, K. (2000). *Stories within and between selves: Identities in relation on the professional knowledge landscape.* Paper-formatted doctoral dissertation, University of Alberta, Edmonton, AB.

Huber, M. (2008). *Narrative curriculum making as identity making: Intersecting family, cultural and school landscapes.* Unpublished doctoral dissertation, University of Alberta, Edmonton, AB.

Huber, M., Clandinin, D. J., & Huber, J. (2006). Relational responsibilities as narrative inquirers. *Curriculum and Teaching Dialogue, 8*(1 & 2), 209–223.

Joe, R. (2000). *We are the dreamers: Recent and early poetry* (Referenced on p. 61 to a poem 'we teach'). Wreck Cove, NS: Breton Books.

King, T. (2003). *The truth about stories: A native narrative.* Minneapolis, MN: University of Minnesota Press.

Kirkness, V., & Barnhardt, R. (1991). First nations and higher education: The four R's – Respect, relevance, reciprocity, responsibility. *Journal of American Indian Education*, *30*(3), 1–14.

Li, Y. (2006). *Where is home: The lived experiences of three Chinese international students in Canada*. Unpublished doctoral dissertation, University of Alberta, Edmonton, AB.

Lindemann Nelson, H. (1995). Resistance and insubordination. *Hypatia*, *10*(2), 23.

Lopez, B. (1993). *Crow and Weasel*. Toronto: Random House of Canada Limited.

Lorde, A. (1984). *Sister outsider: Essays and speeches by Audre Lorde*. Freedom, CA: The Crossing Press.

Lugones, M. (1987). Playfulness, "world"-travelling, and loving perception. *Hypatia*, *2*(2), 3–19.

Marmon Silko, L. (1996). *Yellow woman and a beauty of the spirit: Essays on Native American life today*. New York, NY: Simon & Schuster.

Menzies, C. (2004). Putting words into action: Negotiating collaborative research in Gitxaala. *Canadian Journal of Native Education*, *28*(1 & 2), 15–32.

Menzies, C., Archibald, J., & Smith, G. (Eds.). (2004). Editorial: Transformational sites of Indigenous education*Canadian Journal of Native Education*, *28*(1 & 2), 1–7.

Mi'kmaw Kina'matnewey. (no publication date given). *Mi'maw-English Lexicon: L'nui'sultiney*. Membertou, NS: Mi'kmaw Kina'matnewey.

Mi'kmaw Kina'matnewey. (2000). *AFN post-secondary education review: Nova Scotia and Newfoundland report final report*, Chignecto Consulting Group on behalf of Mi'kmaw Kina'matnewey, Truro, NS.

Miller, J. L. (1998). Autobiography and the necessary incompleteness of teachers' stories. In W. C. Ayers & J. L. Miller (Eds.), *A light in dark times: Maxine Greene and the unfinished conversation* (pp. 145–154). New York, NY: Teachers College Press.

Moore, D. (2001). Validity of native spirituality. Paper presented at St. Michael's College, September 25–26, Colchester, VT.

Moore, D. (2002). Mi'kmaq language a human right. Paper presented at Human Rights Education Conference, Halifax, NS.

Moore, D. (2004). From exclusive to inclusive education. Paper presented at St. Francis Xavier University, Antigonish, NS.

Morris, D. (2002). Narrative, ethics, and pain: Thinking *with* stories. In R. Charon & M. Montello (Eds.), *Stories matter: The role of narrative in medical ethics* (pp. 196–218). New York, NY: Routledge.

Murphy, S. (2004). *Understanding children's knowledge: A narrative inquiry into school experiences*. Unpublished doctoral dissertation, University of Alberta, Edmonton, AB.

Nelson, C. (2003). *'Stories to live by': A narrative inquiry into five teachers' shifting identities through the borderlands of cross-cultural professional development*. Unpublished doctoral dissertation, University of Alberta, Edmonton, AB.

Orr, J., Paul, J. J., & Paul, S. (2002). Decolonizing Mi'kmaq education through cultural practical knowledge. *McGill Journal of Education*, *37*(3), 331–354.

Paley, V. G. (1998). *The girl with the brown crayon: How children use stories to shape their lives*. Cambridge, MA: Harvard University Press.

Pearce, M. (2005). *Telling stories of community: A narrative inquiry into the experiences of a parent and child with/in a school landscape*. Unpublished doctoral dissertation, University of Alberta, Edmonton, AB.

Pryor, B. M. (1998). *Maybe tomorrow*. Ringwood, Victoria, Australia: Penguin Books.

Restoule, J. P. (2000). Aboriginal identity: The need for historical and contextual perspectives. *Canadian Journal of Native Education, 24*(2), 102–111.

Reynolds, P. (2003). *The dot.* Cambridge, MA: Candlewick.

Robertson, D. A., & Blackstone, M. (2008). *The Life of Helen Betty Osborne.* Winnipeg: Portage & Main Press.

Royal Commission on Aboriginal Peoples. (1996). *Report of the Royal Commission on Aboriginal peoples.* Ottawa, ON: Canada Communications Group.

Sarris, G. (1997). The truth will rise. In L. Crozier-Hogle & B. Wilson (Eds.), *Surviving in two worlds: Contemporary Native American voices* (pp. 225–233). Houston, TX: University of Texas Press.

Schwab, J. (1973). The practical 3: Translation into curriculum. *The School Review, 81*(4), 501–522.

St. Denis, V. (2010). *A study of Aboriginal teachers professional knowledge and experience in Canadian schools.* Ottawa, ON: Canadian Council on Learning.

Steeves, P. (2000). *Crazy quilt: Continuity, identity and a storied school landscape in transition. A teacher's and a principal's works in progress.* Unpublished doctoral dissertation, University of Alberta, Edmonton, AB.

Steeves, P. (2004). A place of possibility: The centre for research for teacher education and development. *ATA Magazine, 84*(4), 16–17.

Steeves, P., Yeom, J. S., Pushor, D., Nelson, C., Mwebi, B. M., Murphy, M. S., ... Clandinin, D. J. (2009). The research issues table: A place of possibilities for the education of teacher educators. In C. J. Craig & L. F. Deretchin (Eds.), *Teacher learning in small-group settings: Teacher education yearbook XVII* (pp. 303–320). Toronto, ON: Rowman & Littlefield Education.

Stonechild, B. (2006). *The new buffalo: The struggle for Aboriginal post-secondary education.* Winnipeg, MB: University of Manitoba Press.

Sweetland, W., Huber, J., & Keats Whelan, K. (2004). Narrative inter-lappings: Recognizing difference across tension. *Reflective Practice, 5*(1), 45–74.

The Council of Ministers of Education. (2008, December 12). *Backgrounder of the CMEC Aboriginal education action plan* (pp. 1–4). Toronto, ON. Retrieved from http://www.cmec.ca

Tompkins, J. (2002). Learning to see what they can't: Decolonizing perspectives on Indigenous education in the racial context of rural Nova Scotia. *McGill Journal of Education, 37*(3), 405–422.

Trinh, M. H. (1989). *Woman, native, other.* Indianapolis, IN: Indiana University Press.

Tuhiwai Smith, L. (1999). *Decolonizing methodologies: Research and indigenous peoples.* New York, NY: Zed Books Ltd.

Vinz, R. (1997). Capturing a moving form: "Becoming" as teachers. *English Education, 29*(2), 137–146.

Ward, A., & Bouvier, R. (2001). *Resting lightly on Mother Earth: The Aboriginal experience in urban educational settings.* Calgary, AB: Detselig Enterprises Ltd.

Welsh, C. (1994). *Keepers of the fire (video).* Ottawa, ON: National Film Board of Canada/Omni Film Productions Ltd.

Whelan, K., & Huber, J. (2000). *Stories of self and other: Identities in relation on the professional knowledge landscape.* Paper-formatted doctoral dissertation, University of Alberta, Edmonton, AB.

Wilson, D., & Macdonald, D. (2010). *The income gap between Aboriginal peoples and the rest of Canada*. Ottawa, ON: Canadian Centre for Policy Alternatives.

Young, M. (2005a). Is the legacy of residential schools relevant today? *Manitoba Association of School Superintendents*, Fall, 35–38.

Young, M. (2005b). *Pimatisiwin: Walking in a good way – A narrative inquiry into language as identity*. Winnipeg, MB: Pemmican Publishing Inc..

Young, M., Chester, B. M., Joe, L., Marshall, L., Moore, D., Paul, K., ..., Huber, J. (2008). Composing our lives together. An oral co-presentation of storied inquiry experiences at the Atlantic Native Teacher Education Conference, May 14–16, Membertou, NS.

Young, M., Chester, J. L., Flett, B. M., Joe, L., Marshall, L., Moore, D., ... Huber, J. (2010). Becoming "real" Aboriginal teachers: Attending to intergenerational narrative reverberations and responsibilities. *Teachers and Teaching: Theory and Practice*, 16(3), 285–305.

Young, M. I. (1997). *Anishinabe voice: The cost of education in a non-Aboriginal world*. Unpublished master's thesis, University of Manitoba, Winnipeg, MB.

Young, M. I. (2003). *Pimatisiwin, walking in a good way: A narrative inquiry into language as identity*. Unpublished doctoral dissertation, University of Alberta, Edmonton, AB.

Zhao, G. (2007). *The power of stories: A narrative inquiry into immigrant children's and parents' intergenerational stories of school*. Unpublished doctoral dissertation, University of Alberta, Edmonton, AB.

LEARNING TO SEE THE LITTLE GIRL IN THE MOON: AN AFTERWORD TO WARRIOR WOMEN

It seems only right that I begin to write the Afterword to this book on a night when the full moon is shining down on me. Mary Young taught me long ago about the importance of the moon, and particularly about the little girl in the moon. I have trouble seeing that little girl in the moon but each time the moon becomes round and full, I look for her. She seems to hide from me, to be invisible to me, even though I search for her. Mary tries to help me but only once did I think I caught a glimpse of her.

My search for the little girl in the moon is a search to help me see something, to make it visible to me. Mary tells me she is there and so I know she is. Mary's worlds are different from mine. And I so want to learn from her. Yet I still struggle to see, to really see that little girl, the little girl that Mary tells me is there. And I wait for I know that Mary helps me see many things that I have not seen before, many things that I work still to understand about what it is to live in Mary's worlds and for Mary to learn to live in my worlds. I have learned, slowly, ever so slowly, to world travel to her worlds over many years. While it was not easy for Mary to learn to travel to my worlds, of necessity, she needed to travel to them. Because I inhabit more dominant worlds, I have a choice about whether to travel to Mary's worlds. She does not have a choice about traveling to mine. Her experiences in the residential schools taught her that she must travel to mine. Mary helps me travel to her world, to understand what it is to be her in her worlds. I use the term worlds in the way that Lugones does.

The reason why I think that travelling to someone's 'world' is a way of identifying with them is because by travelling to their 'world' we can [begin to] understand *what it is to be them and what it is to be ourselves in their eyes*. Only when we have traveled to each other's 'worlds' are we fully subject to each other. (Lugones, 1987, p. 17, italics in original)

I have walked alongside Mary for many years now, learning to perceive her with what Lugones calls loving perception, for without loving perception, I "fail to identify with [her] – fail to love [her] – in this particularly deep way" (Lugones, 1987, p. 8). It is travelling to each other's worlds with loving perception that "enables us to be through loving each other" (p. 8).

And Mary and I have learned "to be through loving each other." Through walking alongside her with an openness to how she is constructed and constructs herself, and how I am constructed and how I construct myself, that is, by being in relation, I can travel to her worlds and understand what it is to be her, and what it is to be myself in her eyes. Mary is, as Sean Lessard tells me some teachers are, a gentle teacher. And slowly I have come to see something of her worlds; the way I can come to knowing her worlds is through walking alongside over many years and multiple contexts and through listening with three ears, as Jo-ann Archibald (2008) writes, the two on the sides of my head and the one in my heart.

My gazing at the moon, my search for the little girl in the moon, and my failure to see her is, perhaps, like many silences. Perhaps I could call this a kind of visual silence, the white spaces on the pages of the many texts I read, the photograph that is not there, the words that are blanked out. The silences where I sense, feel, there is more, but I cannot quite see what it is. There are silences where I can listen and continue to try to discern, or silences that I can fill in, color in, with my words and stories. I will never learn to see the little girl in the moon if I continue to fill in the stories with what I already know.

And so I have been patient, and Mary has been patient with me. There are stories that live in silences, so many stories. My search for the stories that live in the silence of not seeing the little girl in the moon is a search of always trying, of wondering, of trying to soften my vision into a kind of peripheral vision (Bateson, 1994) so that I might see her. As I learned to world travel to Mary's worlds, so too did Janice. Through years of sitting together at the Research Issues table, Mary invited Janice and I to travel to her worlds and to hear her stories. We invited Mary to our worlds.

I walked alongside Janice and Mary as they began to imagine this narrative inquiry many years ago and then continued to walk alongside as Khea, Brenda Mary, Lucy, Jennifer, Laura, Jerri-Lynn, Florence, and Sister Dorothy joined the conversation. Now there were many more worlds as each woman inhabited their own unique worlds. I sat and listened, trying to see the little girl in the moon, and trying to hear the stories of the experiences of being, and becoming, teachers of Aboriginal heritage. I joined in,

I listened, I sat in places in multiple cities, I sometimes spoke but rarely for such was my listening that I knew I needed to learn to listen to stories that were not told, that were not visible. These were stories that were not yet visible to me but which I sensed lived everywhere in the multiple worlds of the authors of this book.

Stories like the ones that Anna Neumann (1997) wrote of, the "existence of wordless stories in people's lives" (p. 107). Neumann wrote

> People live their stories as much as they tell them in words. They live them in what they do not say. They live them in attending to the words of others rather than their own. They live them in the gaze that comes with inward thought and inward talk while others all around are conversing. They live them in the feelings that come to surround them, that they give off in sighs and looks and gestures, or simply in the feeling that their presence evokes in others. All of these are forms of telling, though without words, and they are forms of telling that we can begin to read and hear though those also without words. (pp. 107–108)

Slowly, ever so slowly, the stories started to become visible as quietly, in different languages and in different spaces, the stories that had been lived in silences began to be told.

In this lovely book, we read the stories but we also read the temporal unfolding of the struggle to tell in the spaces these courageous women opened up in the relations between researchers, Elders, teachers. These are not easy stories; they are hard to tell stories for they make visible the pain, the hurt, the anger of many years of struggling for narrative coherence (Carr, 1986), as if these institutional, social, and cultural narratives allow for them to achieve narrative coherence. They do not.

While Carr writes,

> Our lives admit of sometimes more, sometimes less coherence; they hang together reasonably well, but they occasionally tend to fall apart. Coherence seems to be a need imposed on us whether we seek it or not. Things need to make sense. We feel the lack of sense when it goes missing. (p. 97)

What Carr does not highlight but which these stories do, is that in becoming visible, we come to understand that many institutional narratives of schooling and post-secondary education are not narratives within which many people of Aboriginal heritage can make sense easily. The struggles for narrative coherence that they experience are more difficult than the struggles for many others. It is only through the making visible that we can begin to understand just how difficult this struggle for narrative coherence has been for these teachers of Aboriginal heritage. In making visible their struggles for narrative coherence, they make visible their stories to live by as becoming Warrior Women who will not settle for silence, or for hoping that others will see their struggles of becoming "real teachers." By breaking their silences, we see their pain, see their hopes, and dreams for all their relations. This book makes visible their stories, no longer hidden but represented on the page.

There is more that is still a silence in the pages of the book, that is, the stories of persistence that these courageous women lived as they stayed relentlessly at the writing of this book and the co-composing of this text. Through experiences of profound illness, of death, of moves, of relationships, of the dissolution of relationships, of degrees, of positions, and of the loss of positions, this group of warrior women stayed at it. They met, they talked, they wrote, they phoned each other, they laughed and cried, and still it mattered to them that these stories are told.

I know that there will be critics. This book is "just stories" some will say. As those imagined critics speak, I am reminded of the words of Leslie Marmon Silko, a Laguna storyteller.

> I will tell you something about stories
> They aren't just entertainment
> Don't be fooled
> They are all we have, you see
> All we have to fight off
> Illness and death. You don't have anything
> If you don't have the stories. (Silko, 1997, p. 2)

Here are the stories of a group of wonderful Warrior Women who created spaces for themselves where they could tell stories of who they are, and are becoming. In their stories, they tell us, if we are listening, of how we might reconfigure the institutional narratives of post-secondary education, and the stories of school, in new ways that would honour the lives of people of Aboriginal heritage, that would open educative spaces for them to become. They are, as King might say, "[s]aving stories, if you will. Stories that will help keep [us] alive" (2003, p. 119).

Mary, I will keep looking for that little girl in the moon for I know that she is there, waiting for me to be able to see her. The courage that the authors of this book show us means that I have a responsibility to keep looking, and to keep changing my stories to live by so that the stories of these courageous women and all their relations can become part of the stories of school and the stories of post-secondary institutions.

Thank you to the authors of this book for allowing us to world travel to your worlds, for making your stories visible. Now it is up to those of us who work in post-secondary education to do something for we have now heard the stories (King, 2003).

D. Jean Clandinin
Centre for Research for Teacher Education and Development
University of Alberta

ABOUT THE CONTRIBUTORS

Janice Huber grew up in Crooked Creek, Alberta in the midst of a family and place that greatly shapes her life. Janice is the mother of one beautiful daughter. As a classroom teacher Janice taught in rural, international, and urban school contexts. Growing from her doctoral and post doctoral study in the late 1990s Janice's collaborative narrative inquiries continue to attend to the lives of children, families, teachers, Elders, and teacher education students in relation with their experiences in home, community, school, and post-secondary places. Janice currently teaches in the Faculty of Education at the University of Regina. She is a coauthor of numerous articles and book chapters, including the two books, *Composing Diverse Identities: Narrative Inquiries into the Interwoven Lives of Children and Teachers* (2006) and *Places of Curriculum Making: Narrative Inquiries into Children's Lives in Motion* (2011).

Lucy Joe grew up and continues to live and teach in the *Mi'kmaq* community of Membertou, Nova Scotia. As the mother of four beautiful children and two beautiful step-children, alongside her work as a Grade 3 teacher at Membertou School and through the support of her husband, Pat Joe, Lucy continues to be passionately engaged in working with children and families in ways that respect the *Mi'kmaq* language and culture and that supports this vital learning for current and future generations of children in the community. Lucy completed her B.Ed. After-Degree at St. Francis Xavier University in Antigonish, Nova Scotia in 2003 and began teaching at Membertou School that fall. In the spring of 2009, Lucy completed her M.Ed. in Leadership and Policy at St. Francis Xavier University and, over the past years, in addition to teaching, serves as the Vice Principal of Membertou School. In 2008 Lucy was nominated by her colleagues for the Prime Minister's Award for Teaching Excellence.

Jennifer Lamoureux (*née Williams*) is an elementary school teacher in Winnipeg, Manitoba. She currently teaches Grade 5 students and lives with her husband, who is also an educator at the post-secondary level, and her cat, Mandy, and dog, Winnie. Coming from mixed Aboriginal heritage in a non-Aboriginal community, Jennifer believes there is a need for more teachers of Aboriginal descent. In addition to her goals of building efficacy in students with Aboriginal ancestry, she aims to foster positive connections between all students and their school experience.

Laura Marshall (*Lulu*) is in her ninth year of teaching at Eskasoni Elementary Middle School in the *Mi'kmaq* community of Eskasoni, Nova Scotia. She is the mother of four beautiful teenagers who are each central in her knowing as a teacher as was her husband of 18 years, *Atji*, who recently passed. While growing up in Eskasoni Laura was privileged by the time she spent with her grandparents who taught her to both know and to be proud of the *Mi'kmaq* language and culture. Her dream of becoming a teacher of *Mi'kmaq* language and culture shaped Laura's completion of her B.Ed. After-Degree at St. Francis Xavier University in Antigonish, Nova Scotia in 2003. In the fall of 2008, Laura completed her M.Ed. in Curriculum and Instruction at St. Francis Xavier University during which she wrote the research project, *Narrative Accounts of Life in Grades Eight and Nine Mi'kmaq Language Classrooms.*

Sister Dorothy Moore is an educator, human rights activist, and *Mi'kmaq* Elder from Membertou, Nova Scotia. She was awarded the Order of Nova Scotia in 2003 and the Order of Canada in 2005 for her life-long commitments and substantial contributions to the equitable education of children, youth, and adults of *Mi'kmaq* and First Nations ancestry, for which she was also earlier honored through awards from the Atlantic Canada Plus Association, the Atlantic Provinces Economic Council, and a citation for Citizenship from the Governor General. Born in Membertou in 1933, Sister Dorothy became the first *Mi'kmaq* of Nova Scotia to be inducted into a Roman Catholic religious order, the Sisters of St. Martha, in Antigonish, Nova Scotia. In her work as an educator, Sister Dorothy taught in Nova Scotia and Alberta, served as principal of Eskasoni School in Eskasoni, Nova Scotia, and played a vital role in the establishment of the current *Mi'kmaq* Resources Centre at Cape Breton University, Sydney, Nova Scotia when she was on faculty there. In addition, she has held key positions in the Nova Scotia Department of Education and the Nova Scotia Human Rights Commission. Sister Dorothy continues to be deeply involved on a variety of education and human rights boards and in initiatives in Nova Scotia and across Canada. Through this narrative inquiry, Sister Dorothy has journeyed deeply with each person, generously and thoughtfully sharing her insights and wisdom. She has been a significant guide to Janice.

Chloe Mustooch (Siktahtoh), the artist who created the moon image on the front cover is a young Stoney woman from Alexis First Nation. She is currently attending Emily Carr University of Art and Design on Granville Island in British Columbia, Canada. Before leaving Edmonton, Chloe was a mentor to many First Nations youth within her home community and the local school system. She is very traditional in her belief systems and her name on the bottom of the painting is Blue Bird in her language; the name was gifted to her when she was born at ceremony.

Jerri-Lynn Orr (*née Chester*) recently completed the Aboriginal Languages Bachelor of Education at the University of Winnipeg, after 2 years of study at Red River College. She and her husband, Stan, are proud parents of their three children, Dennis, who is 9; Andrew, who is 7; and Monique, who is 11 months. Jerri-Lynn grew up in Winnipeg and knew that she wanted to become a teacher at a very young age because of her experiences as a child in Grade 4. At that time, Jerri-Lynn was in foster care and had a teacher who was attentive in her life and cared that she succeeded. She enrolled in the Aboriginal Languages Bachelor of Education Program so she could learn more about her culture and heritage. It was then that she discovered who she was as a *Cree-Metís* woman. She has since become passionate about learning more about her culture so that she will be able to pass this knowledge on to her children and to the children she will teach. In joining with the research group in Winnipeg, she has learned about the experience of life as an Aboriginal educator through the lens of 10 unique, kind, passionate, and knowledgeable women. This experience has helped her to see education as an integral part of nurturing our Aboriginal and non-Aboriginal children and youth so they will know who they are and what they can become.

Brenda Mary Parisian Thunderbird Sounding from the West Woman I am from the Turtle Clan and my *Ogitchita* is the Eagle is of the Star People from Peguis First Nation. I am currently working toward completing 60 credits toward B.Ed. In 2011–2012 I worked as an Education Assistant for Peguis Central School. Brenda believes her calling is to learn the language and teach the history of her people and teach it to students at the school and community. It is her way of empowering herself to decolonize the effects of residential schools which affect all first nation people in one way or another. Attended Peguis Adult Ed. Receiving Development Studies to enter Assiniboine Community College to receive a Diploma for Aboriginal Community Development, and certificate Community Social Development. Attended Red River College to receive Diploma for Aboriginal Language Specialist. Mother of 4 children, 17 grandchildren, and 7 great-grandchildren. I want to show the ones behind me it's never too late to do something positive with yourself – you are learning everyday and life is a teacher.

190 ABOUT THE CONTRIBUTORS

Khea Paul grew up in the *Mi'kmaq* community of Eskasoni, Nova Scotia where she is now raising three beautiful daughters. Khea is in her 16th year of teaching. During her first years in the classroom Khea taught Grade 8 Math and Science at Eskasoni Elementary Middle School. She is currently teaching Grade 10 Math at Allison Bernard Memorial High School, Eskasoni. Khea completed her B.Ed. degree at Dalhousie University in Halifax, Nova Scotia in the spring of 1993. In the fall of 2008 Khea graduated from St. Francis Xavier University in Antigonish, Nova Scotia with her M.Ed. in Leadership and Policy. Beyond teaching and being a mother, Khea is significantly involved in the Eskasoni community through crisis intervention work.

Florence Paynter hails from Sandy Bay First Nation and holds a band membership from Norway House First Nation. Florence is a long time educator and started her educational career in the early 1970s. She has been a classroom teacher, a consultant, and an instructor at the university level. Florence is the co-founder of the Manitoba Association of Languages, now called the Aboriginal Languages of Manitoba. She has helped design and has delivered First Nations Languages Programs. She was instrumental in having the First Nations Languages recognized for high school credit. She worked for the province of Manitoba as a consultant for Aboriginal education for several years. In 2000, she joined the Manitoba First Nations Education Resource Centre as the Coordinator of the Aboriginal Language Initiative initially and is now the Coordinator of the Research and Development Unit. Florence speaks her language fluently and is an active participant of the traditional ways of the *Anishinabe* people. She holds a Masters Degree in Education. Florence has been asked to be the Elder representative for several research projects and development work at the university level and sits with the students becoming researchers and teachers in this narrative inquiry.

Mary Isabelle Young is *Anishinabe Kwe* from Bloodvein First Nation. She received her early education, Grades 1–8, in Bloodvein, Manitoba. She attended residential school for 3 years and graduated from Kelvin High School in Winnipeg. She obtained her Bachelor of Arts from the University of Winnipeg, Post-Baccalaureate in Education and Masters of Education from the University of Manitoba. She completed her Ph.D. in First Nations Education from the University of Alberta. Notwithstanding these degrees, Mary consistently honors the ways her parents taught and educated her. She believes they were truly her first teachers. Her parents were the ones who encouraged her and insisted she speaks *Anishinabemowin*. In 1984 Mary began as a Native Student Advisor and became the first Director of the Aboriginal Student Services Centre at the University of Winnipeg. She is currently an Assistant Professor in the Faculty of Education at the University of Winnipeg.

CPSIA information can be obtained
at www.ICGtesting.com
Printed in the USA
LVOW13s1745290718

585290LV00015B/1047/P